The Art of Learning a Foreign Language

25 Things I Wish They Told Me

BENJAMIN BATARSEH

Thanks to my family for instilling the value of education and to the many excellent teachers I have had over the years. Also, special thanks to my friend and Harvard Graduate, Daniel Yarbrough, for providing detailed feedback on the original manuscript.

CONTENTS

INTRODUCTION..9

Chapter 1

Choose Your Target Language Wisely..................11

Chapter 2

To Study A Foreign Language Is To Become A Child...22

Chapter 3

What You Study in the Classroom Is Not What People Speak on the Street.....................................25

Chapter 4

Studying Grammar and Looking up Words You Don't Know Improves Your Language Skills Exponentially...30

Chapter 5

Avoid Burnout by Making Friends in the Target Language and Engaging in Passive Language Activities..34

Chapter 6

Your Native Language Ability Influences Your Potential in a Foreign Language...........................39

Chapter 7

Learning A Foreign Language Improves Linguistic Creativity...42

Chapter 8

*The More Foreign Languages You Know,
The Easier It Is To Learn New Ones*......................45

Chapter 9

*When Traveling, Country, Occupation, and
Lifestyle Influence Language Learning Outcomes*
....49

Chapter 10

*Your Pronunciation Influences People's Perception
of Your Language Skills*..56

Chapter 11

*You Improve Your Pronunciation by Listening in
the Target Language and Clearing Chronic
Tension From the Voice* 59

Chapter 12

*Learning A Foreign Language May Change Your
Personality* 66

Chapter 13

*Learning A Foreign Language May Make You Less
Popular*...71

Chapter 14

*Language Immersion in the 21st Century Is
Possible Wherever You Are*...................................74

Chapter 15

Atomic Habit #1: Thinking in the Target Language
....79

Chapter 16

Atomic Habit #2: Interpretation in the Target Language 85

Chapter 17

Atomic Habit #3: Leveraging Screentime in the Target Language 91

Chapter 18

Embrace Being Corrected as a Means of Progress 95

Chapter 19

Progress in a Foreign Language Should Be Measured in Hours, Not Months or Years 99

Chapter 20

Linguistic "Muscle Memory" Is A Real Thing 102

Chapter 21

Having Clear Foreign Language Goals Maximizes Output 108

Chapter 22

Context Is Key to Understanding Any Communication 112

Chapter 23

Music, Comedy, and Dialogue Test Advanced Listening Proficiency 117

Chapter 24

Your Relationship to the Target Language Will Evolve 125

Chapter 25

Foreign Language Study Is Not A Silver Bullet for the World's Problems 128

CONCLUSION 132

ABOUT THE AUTHOR 133

REFERENCES 134

INTRODUCTION

Language is the gateway to culture and the riches of humanity thereof. It affords access to people, history, ideas, art, religion, aesthetics, and economic opportunities. Language also exerts a transformative effect on the vessel through whom it is expressed. Charlemagne is reported to have said that "To speak another language is to possess another soul."[1]

The Art of Learning a Foreign Language consists of all the things I wish I knew at various stages of my language learning journey during the last 15 years—as a hobbyist, student, academic, and professional linguist. This book is designed to help the learner avoid many pitfalls and seize opportunities, with lessons on choosing a target language, travel, accent, immersion, technology, learning approaches, and the lifestyle habits of professional linguists.

Some of the chapters address topics of general interest to the language learner ("nice to know"). Other headings address more crucial issues with potentially vast implications for the language learner ("must know"). Had I known then what I know now, I would have made some different choices, but the beauty of life is that it can be lived in only one direction.

In sum, with unprecedented language learning resources at our disposal and abundant opportunities for cross-cultural connection, today is the most exciting time in history to acquire proficiency in a foreign language. Whatever your motivations for learning a foreign language—or current foreign language level—this digestible read will bring you closer to achieving your goals.

I strove to organize this book in a logical fashion by progressively incorporating more advanced concepts, but it can be read any way you find helpful. You can proceed from beginning to end or skip around as needed. While many of the points apply to all languages, the examples I use are naturally taken from the languages with which I have experience.

Chapter 1

Choose Your Target Language Wisely

According to Ethnologue, a widely cited annual research publication on the living languages of the world, there are currently 7,151 spoken languages today,[2] let alone "dead languages," like Latin, Biblical Hebrew, and Akkadian. In a world powered by the internet and overflowing with formal educational opportunities, there is no shortage of target languages to choose. This is a prime example of Barry Schwartz's "paradox of choice," where having a surplus of options, which is generally considered to be a good thing, can increase stress and paralyze decision-makers.[3] Naturally, the extent and scope of an individual's language goals, and their corresponding level of commitment, determine how high the stakes are for selecting the right target language. As with any other decision, it makes sense to invest a proportionate amount of time in the decision-making process. Below, I outline some guiding principles and practical considerations that can lay the framework for a successful experience.

Know Your "Why"

The first step in selecting a target language is to identify your motivation. For example, culture is a powerful motivation for many language learners. The ranks of college language classes are filled with "heritage speakers," defined as students with an informal background in a second language that was spoken in their home. Heritage speakers enroll in language classes to gain literacy and develop in the four basic language skills (reading, writing, speaking, and listening). It is also common for "heritage learners" to study a language they are ethnically or historically connected to, even if they did not grow up speaking it. For example, I decided to take Arabic in college because of my family's Jordanian ancestry, and I had classmates with ethnic roots in Iraq and Lebanon.

Where heritage is not a factor, the culturally motivated may desire to learn about a people, history, or religion; connect with friends; communicate with locals on an international trip; or immerse themselves in a particular subculture. People with an interest in Christianity, Islam, Judaism, and Hinduism may study Ancient Greek, Classical Arabic, Hebrew, and Hindi. In the same way, aficionados of reggaeton, literature, or poetry may begin studying Spanish, French, or Persian. I chose to study Spanish in high school because I had Hispanic friends, was enamored with the sound of the language, and knew there were abundant opportunities to engage with Latin culture both locally and abroad.

Culturally motivated learners can begin their search by exploring avenues of cultural fulfillment. In addition to aesthetic interest and abstract attraction to a language, which are meaningful considerations, we can pose a series of practical questions to guide our thinking. E.g. What is it I love about this language? Do I plan on living in a country where this language is spoken? If not, are there adequate native speakers to connect with remotely or in the local work and cultural spaces I envision myself? How do my cultural prospects with this language compare to those of other languages I am necessarily passing up in the process? Probability is the essence of all sound decision-making. No one has a crystal ball into the future, but we can infer probability based on our prospective life path and what we presently know to be true about ourselves. As new information pours in, we adapt our calculus accordingly.

I think the biggest thing about speaking languages is that more opportunities are going to come your way. In business, even if you only speak one language, you have to perform, right? Like, if you're going to be a successful businessperson, you've got to do what you say you're going to do. You've got to be creative. You've got to provide a benefit to your business partners. But if you have more languages, more potential opportunities are going to come your way. (Steve Kauffman)[4]

For the business and professionally minded, it is beneficial to research current job and career opportunities for people with target language skills and the direction of future trends. The chances are that if you are beginning your language study today, the economic landscape won't be vastly different just a few years down the road. However, do you plan on staying in one location or moving to another city or country, where the economic landscape is different? The most advisable thing anyone can do is talk to experienced language learners and knowledgeable people in the business world. These types usually have insight into questions like these and can spotlight considerations that didn't even occur to us.

As an undergraduate at Georgetown, I took intensive Japanese and Arabic classes for two years. After studying abroad in Tokyo, I decided to drop Japanese to focus on Arabic and Spanish, the latter of which I had been studying independently for years. In reality, while I had a clear gameplan with Arabic and Spanish from the outset, I had no real concept of application with Japanese, nor the economic and cultural realities I was walking into. I thought Japanese was cool-looking and cool-sounding (I still do). I thought it would be nice to diversify my skills by studying an East Asian language (maybe it would have been).

However, in hindsight, these were not good reasons for taking on a commitment so large, given that I wouldn't have been content with anything less than an advanced level of proficiency. I did not intend to move to Japan or work a job in Japanese. I did not even grow up watching anime or reading manga. How did I plan to keep my language skills fresh, and in what domain would knowledge of Japanese be relevant to my life? Common sense, but you'd be surprised how infrequently many learners reflect on questions like these when choosing a target language. Had I followed the advice prescribed in the previous paragraphs, maybe I would have taken a class or two in Japanese rather than a plethora, and not dedicated so much of my free time outside of class to kanji flash cards and verb conjugation charts.

Finally, and perhaps most telling, the reality of how much time it takes to "master" a language as difficult as Japanese gradually dawned on me. Before setting a goal, it is vital to have a concept of how long it will take to achieve, which leads me to my next and most important point.

Data on Language-Learning Milestones

Most beginners predictably have no idea how long it will take to progress in their target language, nor of the relative difficulty of foreign languages depending on their mother tongue. I always wondered why no teacher ever kicked off their introductory language class by addressing the elephant in the room. In the past, maybe good statistics were not available. Or maybe teachers don't want to intimidate students who may already be feeling overwhelmed. However, as I will explain below, I believe that the data can inspire learners and motivate them to set realistic goals. And, in most cases, the commitment required may be well within reach.

On the topic of language-learning milestones, my favorite source to cite is research published by the Foreign Service Institute (FSI), which has been responsible for training American diplomats in foreign languages for over 70 years. The research consists of estimates, or averages, of how many classroom hours of instruction it takes for a learner to achieve "professional working proficiency," which amounts to "Speaking-3/Reading-3" (out of 5) on the Interagency Language Roundtable scale.[5] When the FSI uses the term *proficiency*, this is the level that they are referring to. The estimates, or averages, are based on four levels of languages, in ascending degrees of difficulty. As for the precise time it takes an individual to become proficient, it will vary based on factors like aptitude, experience, and initiative. While the data apply most directly to native English speakers, they may be instructive for all language learners, regardless of their background.

For example, the FSI estimates that it will take 600-750 classroom hours to achieve professional working proficiency for level I languages most similar to English, including French, Spanish, Italian, and Portuguese. The figure for level II languages, including German, Swahili, and Indonesian, is 900 classroom hours. The figure for level III languages, including Russian, Hebrew, Turkish, and Hindi, is 1100 classroom hours. And, finally, the figure for level IV languages, aka the "super hard languages," which consists exclusively of Arabic, Chinese, Japanese, and Korean, is 2200 hours. That's right, it is estimated to take almost *four* times as long to become proficient in a level IV language than a level I language. Note that these figures are for the standard variety of languages, and do not consider local dialects or informal speech, which may differ considerably depending on the language.

Statistics give pause to prospective language learners, but they also inspire and motivate. Maybe a language learner's goal is to reach a level 2 of 5 ("limited working proficiency"), in which case it won't take as long as they anticipated. Or maybe their goal is to reach a level 4 or 5 before pivoting to informal variants, in which case it might take much longer. I know several people who studied a level IV language for years, even majored in it, and still struggle to make their way around in social situations. In cases where the program is not intensive and students do not log a lot of independent work, this is a very typical outcome.

However, the payoff for learning a more difficult language may be greater, depending on where you live. For example, the US government has marked select languages as "critical languages," in terms of US political and economic interests. Critical languages are languages for which there is a great need for professionals, but relatively few speakers to meet it. The current list of critical languages includes all level IV languages, and a handful of level II and level III languages, as well. Critical languages typically pay out a premium for services due to basic supply and demand dynamics.

In any case, data like these are an asset. They enable the learner to formulate detailed study plans based on their individual goals and time horizon. If I know that it will take me roughly 1000 hours to achieve my goal, then I can think of it in terms of an hour a day for three years. Or three hours a day for one year. Now that doesn't sound so intimidating. I can also hold myself accountable based on a specific benchmark rather than a vague notion of progress. In addition, psychology plays a big role in language learning, as you will gather by the end of the book. The closer our expectations line up with reality, the more likely we are to be successful in the long run.

The last input in the decision to study a target language is the availability of coursework and learning materials for that language. In the US, just about every major college offers classes on popular languages, like French, Spanish and German. However, students in the US may have to do some digging to find a reputable program for less popular languages, like Arabic, Japanese, and Swahili. If a learner wants to go the independent route, there are a wealth of resources to choose from. As of the time of this writing, Duo Lingo supports ~19 languages, whereas Rosetta Stone supports ~25. HelloTalk, one of the most popular language exchange applications, is compatible with ~125 languages. I have never used Duo Lingo or Rosetta Stone, but many people swear by them. On the other hand, I have used HelloTalk to converse with native speakers.

Aside from major software applications, the increased quality of online and print resources has changed the game for self-starters. I'm talking about dictionaries, grammars, references, and communities that function much like a teacher or native speaker would in times past. These resources are what enabled me to learn Spanish independently ("por mi propia cuenta") before I ever enrolled in a formal course. Depending on your target language, these resources may be of excellent quality, or they may leave much to be desired.

Finally, I will note that most learners function better in a structured environment. Regular lessons and feedback from a teacher and physical proximity to other like-minded people can accelerate progress and keep emotional interest high. It's the same reason people go to the gym and hire a trainer even if they can do the same workout at home. In sum, the personality and drive of the language learner, in addition to the specific concerns of a target language, dictate how much formal instruction is necessary to achieve one's goals.

Chapter 2

To Study A Foreign Language Is To Become A Child

Personality, in any social context, is largely a function of communication skills. Knowledge, wit, humor, eloquence, and style are all for naught until a learner can activate them in the target language. In an episode of *Modern Family*, Gloria captured the frustration language learners often feel at not being able to fully express themselves: *Do you even know how smart I am in Spanish? Of course you don't.*[6] Learning a second language, it follows, is an exercise in humility.

I spent the summer of 2014 in Nizwa, Oman, studying Arabic on a Critical Language Scholarship sponsored by the US Department of State. As part of the program, you had to sign a pledge where you would only speak Arabic for the entire two months. Everyone privately reneged after the first week, but Arabic was still ubiquitous. The immersive environment was particularly challenging for beginner and intermediate students for obvious reasons. I recall there were PhDs, academics, and professionals with excellent communication skills in English and an unmistakable sense of humor who fell into this category. Observing some of their interactions with the locals, I couldn't help but think to myself, "The locals have no idea what these people are really like."

When you try something new, you're always a fool. And so unless you're willing to be a fool, you can't learn anything new. (Jordan B. Peterson)[7]

Fear of appearing stupid, ignorant, or childish is a nemesis of learning, and language learning is no exception. Frustration is inevitable, but it doesn't have to be final. It's always a letdown when a language learner loses motivation, stops engaging in the target language, or abandons the endeavor altogether. It follows that learning how to manage our emotions and take a long view of situations (i.e., "respect the process") is critical to weathering the storms of acquiring a new skill. Like a baby learning how to walk, we deserve credit for every milestone we attain and for mustering the courage to confront the unknown.

Overall, I like to think of the drop-off in personality inherent to foreign language study as supplemental motivation. I set a goal for myself

years ago to have basically one consistent personality, independent of the language I'm
speaking. This is always an unlikely outcome,
especially when a third or fourth language is
concerned. However, once an advanced level
has been reached, the comfort factor increases,
even if the learner continues to favor their native
language.

Chapter 3

What You Study in the Classroom Is Not What People Speak on the Street

Learners typically begin with the standard variant, that is, the formal variant of a language. This is the advisable route, in most cases, for several reasons. First, we live in the age of writing; the language and grammar characteristic of writing are prevalent in culture. College, in general, is writing- and reading-intensive, and language class is no exception. Second, the standard variant serves as a strong foundation for non-standard/informal variants. I know this to be true of English and the Romance languages (French, Italian, Spanish, Portuguese, etc.) It is also true of Arabic, even though Arabic dialects are substantially different from the standard formal variety in both grammar and vocabulary.

Third, most beginner students wouldn't have a clue which informal variant to begin with. For example, if I'm studying Arabic, would I begin with Egyptian, whose media industry is famous throughout the Arabic world? What about Levantine Arabic, spoken by Jordanians, Palestinians, Syrians, and Lebanese? Or how about Gulf Arabic and the numerous dialects endemic to that region? In the case of Spanish, Mexican dialects, for example, are materially different from those of the Caribbean (Puerto Rico, Dominican Republic, Cuba, coastal South America, etc.) Narrow interests and attachments within a major language landscape often take time to develop. As a result, it makes sense for most new language learners to begin with the standard variant. The standard variant applies to a wide variety of contexts, including business and education, and can later be used as a base to pivot to something more specialized.

Pivoting from Standard to Slang Speech

Continuity notwithstanding, the largish differences between formal and informal variants can be a real wake-up call. Advanced learners may be alarmed to discover that they have a hard time understanding colloquial conversations, especially when the speakers are not "scaling it back" to be understood by foreigners. Informal speech has its own grammar, vocabulary, and intonation, and studying it can often feel like learning an additional language. This is especially true of "diglossic" languages like Arabic and Greek, where, by definition, the differences between the formal and informal variants are quite vast. My family did not speak a great deal of Arabic growing up, and I spent several solid years studying formal Arabic (Fusha) before transitioning to Levantine Arabic. My background in Fusha gave me a leg up, but it still took me several hundred hours of dedicated study to make significant progress with the dialect. Chinese dialects and Swiss German similarly have a reputation for differing greatly from the mainstream.

In the same way, when I was a freshman in college, I passed two out of three sections of the DELE C2 Spanish exam (Diploma de Español como Lengua Extranjera), which assesses the highest level of proficiency in standard Spanish. The exam was administered in D.C. a few times each year and it took around six months for the results to come back in the mail. I remember I passed the oral part, the written and auditory comprehension part, and miserably failed the integrated skills part, where you had to conduct a write-up on various graphs that I could not make sense of for the life of me. I didn't end up getting the certificate, which was disappointing. That said, I was pretty good at standard Spanish early on, and I continued to get better as an undergraduate. However, I discovered that my experience did not always translate to the informal domain. While people with a standard foreign language background may have no problem understanding a newsreel, lecture, debate, sermon, match, article, or publication, they may struggle–as I did–to understand native speakers in their natural element.

Today, I have years of experience studying Mexican and Caribbean dialects, and I am still learning new words all the time. Spanish, like Arabic, has over twenty countries that speak the same language officially. While the divergence of Spanish dialects from the standard form of the language pales in comparison to the Arabic case, the distinctions are not trivial. In addition, informal speech is fast-evolving. Staying current with slang that is in circulation at a particular time and place requires effort.

In sum, the standard version of a language is the ideal place for most beginners to start, whether or not they have an interest in nonstandard speech. Learners who have an interest in non-standard speech are advised to research the formal-informal dynamic of their target language. In this fashion, they can budget their study time accordingly and avoid unpleasant surprises down the road in cases where the differences are exaggerated.

Chapter 4

Studying Grammar and Looking up Words You Don't Know Improves Your Language Skills Exponentially

A dubious theory I hear get recycled regularly is that it isn't necessary or advisable for language learners to study grammar or consult dictionaries. Proponents of this theory hold that the best way to learn a foreign language is to imitate how people naturally learn their native language, that is, through passive exposure in an immersive environment. It is certainly possible to learn a foreign language this way. I imagine this is how most people learned languages before resources were available. However, I also believe this approach is generally the hardest, slowest, and least efficient way for people to go about it in the 21st century. Grammars and dictionaries are invaluable resources that expand horizons and save time that would otherwise be squandered trying to reinvent the wheel.

It does not follow that the best way for an adult to learn a foreign language is the same way a child learns their native language. A child's brain is wired differently than an adult brain.

Children are capable of passively absorbing language through contact, whereas adults require instruction.[8] The brilliance of this process aside, native speakers don't have a chronological advantage. Most adult learners wouldn't be content to speak a foreign language like a native 8-year-old, 12-year-old, or even a 16-year-old. With a fully developed brain, worldly experience, and educational resources, adults can learn foreign languages in a much more time-efficient manner (albeit, with a lot more conscious effort), than they learned their native languages growing up.

An active learning approach is energy-intensive—asking questions, looking up words, studying things. A passive learning approach, on the other hand, is energy-*un*intensive. A passive learning approach is when we watch a movie in the target language, the majority of which we cannot understand, without subtitles or a dictionary. A passive learning approach is when we nod and smile when we don't understand something in conversation instead of directing questions to the speaker. Learning, to be sure, is about what we retain in our minds, not what passes through our ears and our eyes. While a passive learning approach may work well for children, it is needlessly fruitless for adults. In contrast, under an active learning approach, we learn more, and we learn faster. While this principle applies most notably to beginner and intermediate learners, it remains true for advanced learners.

Moreover, trying to deduce the meaning of words from context and generalize grammatical rules based on specific examples (inductive reasoning) often leads to inaccurate or imprecise conclusions. That isn't to suggest that inferences are irrelevant or that we should never make them. On the contrary, the skill of inference is something I've tried to develop for years, frequently replaying audio and pondering the meaning of new words in writing. However, it's constructive to consult a reference at the end of this process. This enables us to "check our work" and have the certainty to add new words to our active vocabulary.

Every dictionary entry or grammar rule worth its salt is complete with example sentences. Example sentences reinforce, contextualize, and activate; they inspire confidence, as per above, and keep the learner from making silly mistakes. In addition to example sentences, this chapter is premised on abundant exposure to the target language via reading, listening, speaking, and writing. Indeed, these activities are what prompt most word look-ups and grammar consultations.

It follows that the more language input we feed ourselves with, and the more language output we generate, the more relevant the question becomes of whether to look things up. To be sure, it is not advisable to look up words, ask questions, and read example sentences all the time. This process exhausts the learner emotionally (see chapter 5 for more on morale). However, as a rule, the more actively the learner engages with the unknown, the faster their language level improves.

To sum it up bluntly, the choice to regularly look up new words and phrases or consult a teacher or native speaker with doubts, on one hand... or the choice to passively "go with the flow," trying to infer the meaning of everything new by context or ignoring it outright, on the other hand... may be the difference between becoming proficient within a few years and spending an entire lifetime bumbling around in a target language. I say that because I've been involved in language learning communities long enough to see this distinction play out a hundred times. The dictionary (human or otherwise) isn't *just* for nerds like me. It's for all serious language learners who want to accelerate progress.

Chapter 5

Avoid Burnout by Making Friends in the Target Language and Engaging in Passive Language Activities

In an interview with Forbes, American author of *Mastery* and multilingual, Robert Greene, was asked about "the secret ingredients to becoming a world master at something."[9] Greene's response, which applies to learning in general, underscores the pivotal role of psychology in the process:

> *We all know how much more deeply we learn when we are motivated. If a subject excites us, if it stirs our deepest curiosity, or if we have to learn because the stakes are high, we pay much more attention. What we absorb sinks in. If we find ourselves in France needing to learn the language, or suddenly in love with a French woman who speaks little English, we can learn more in a few months than four years of French classes, no matter how good the teacher. In*

other words, our level of focus will determine the depth of our learning. (Robert Greene)

There will doubtlessly be days when we don't feel motivated to do the grunt work necessary to make progress in a language. That is when discipline comes into play. However, all things equal, motivation is a great asset to have. That is because, as Greene articulated in a recent segment on language learning, "The mind is more receptive when you're excited, when you're liking something, when you're interested in it."[10] Speaking for myself, passion is what has kept me consistent with my language studies, independent of where I was living, whether I was taking classes, whether my job required foreign language proficiency, and how many target language connections I had at the time.

Language, as I described in the introductory chapter, is the gateway to a culture. It confers access to the realms of people, economics, and ideas, and it possesses artistic and aesthetic qualities. Maybe one or more of these factors is what inspired you to study a foreign language. As for me, the potential for human relationships was my primary motivation. In high school, I would study computer programming languages in my free time. I founded a general discussion board that grew to over 5,000 members. However, the process was often solitary and left me with serious questions about the kind of lifestyle this work entailed. One day, I vividly remember deciding to channel my general passion for languages into a tool for fostering the people-to-people connections that I valued. I scrapped the PHP coding manual I had printed from the internet, started the process of closing my website, and took up a newfound interest in spoken languages.

To this day, routine interactions with friends, family, teachers, colleagues, and associates from target language communities energize my interest in foreign languages. With regards to the human element, I am the rule, not the exception. This phenomenon also applies to learners of "dead languages," like Latin, Coptic, and Ancient Greek, who explore human-related affairs and foster community among like-minded people.

The Pitfalls of a Hyperactive Language Approach

In addition to the human element, curriculum and methodology influence the psychology of language learning success. In the previous chapter, I shared my belief that an *active* approach maximally facilitates learning. Simply put, we learn faster when we engage intensively with the unknown. That said, there is wisdom in not going overboard with this, given the psycho-emotional factor at play. I understand as much as anyone how mentally exhausting it can be to study definitions and grammar ad nauseam. I've spent thousands of hours in my lifetime studying dry vocabulary lists and reading plain dictionary entries, often in absurdly small font. (I attribute some of my near-sightedness to this, although who really knows.) Too much tedious activity can leave the learner feeling demoralized. In general, people whose only activities in a foreign language are dense run a greater risk of burnout. Over time, they may even lose interest altogether. For this reason, it is advisable to regularly engage with friends in the target language and consume stimulating content as much as possible.

Burnout is also why *passive* language learning activities can sometimes be very beneficial. For example, relaxing to a song, movie, book, or conversation in a target language without looking up any words or preoccupying the mind with linguistic minutiae. In these moments, learners can focus on mastering what they already know. As for the unknown, they can draw inferences based solely on context without racking their brains. Passive language activities are doubly productive when learners have acquired a solid language base, without which their ability to rehearse, refine, and infer is constrained.

Motivation depends on the nature of activity, but it also depends on perceptions of progress. When we see that we are making good progress in a language, we may feel inspired to compound the effect. In sum, we want to balance our big picture desire for maximum learning with our shorter-term need for emotional stimulation. The onus is on the language learner to determine how much active and passive language activity is appropriate for them on any given day.

Chapter 6

Your Native Language Ability Influences Your Potential in a Foreign Language

This section reminds me of a famous Ted Talk given by Suzanne Talhouk in Beirut (2012).[11] In it, Talhouk lamented the devaluement of Arabic by many of her fellow Lebanese, who preferred to speak English or French as a show of "contemporariness" and "civilization." Talhouk attributed this phenomenon to the diminished importance of Arabic at school, work, research labs, and airports. I know a lot of people in non-Arabic speaking countries can also relate. However, Talhouk discussed the cultural, national, and existential reasons why cherishing and protecting one's native language is important. Talhouk also cited studies indicating that one's level of mastery over their native language influences their ability to become proficient in foreign ones. This critical point, which is often lost on people who depreciate their native language, is the focus of this chapter.

Imagine that you must learn thirty vocabulary items in your target language. Now imagine that you already know the meaning of these words in your native language. For example, if you know the word *repetitive* means *something that is repeated excessively*, you can jump directly to the corresponding word *repetitivo* in Spanish. This task may take you roughly a half hour, depending on your level of focus and how deeply you want to commit the items to memory.

On the other hand, imagine you must learn thirty vocabulary items in your target language, but this time you don't have any idea what they mean in your native language. Now, in addition to the spelling and sound, you need to memorize the definition. For example, let's say you don't know that the word *polarizing (polarizante)* means *highly controversial* and that *kiosk (quiosco)* refers to *a small stand where information is provided or items are sold*. In this second case, it may take you roughly two hours to learn the thirty items, depending on how difficult the definitions are. It follows that being able to "flip the switch" from one's native language to a foreign language makes for maximum efficiency and prevents having to learn everything from the ground up. Indeed, strong native language skills drastically reduce the time it takes to gain proficiency as the learner repeats this process many times over.

In the same manner, worldly knowledge, critical thinking skills, and linguistic creativity quickly convert into a target language as soon as they are given a vehicle for expression. A 24-year-old, for example, who traveled, went to college, and gained life experience has a much higher linguistic ceiling than the 16-year-old version of themselves. While they both start from square one, the one with stronger native language skills is going to progress further and faster.

Chapter 7

Learning A Foreign Language Improves Linguistic Creativity

"You can never understand one language until you understand at least two." (Geoffrey Willans)[12]

This idea is not easy to rationalize or explain, especially to someone who has never studied a foreign language. But I believe improved linguistic creativity merits its own chapter, given how profoundly I have been able to appreciate the effect in my personal experience. Indeed, I identify improved linguistic creativity as one of the most compelling legacies of foreign language study.

When you begin learning a foreign language, you do not possess an advanced vocabulary. One of the most obvious effects of an advanced vocabulary is streamlined communication. For example, the word *intelligent* may denote *someone with a high mental capacity*. Now imagine that you did not know what the word *intelligent* meant, and you had to say the full sentence *someone with a high mental capacity* every single time you wanted to refer to an intelligent person. Or take, for example, the word *prima donna*. When we call someone a *prima donna*, we mean *someone who is high-maintenance or has an inflated ego*. What if you didn't know what *high-maintenance* and *inflated ego* meant? You get my point – that vocabulary, for all its creative and phonetic merits, has the practical effect of streamlining communication.

When a learner without an advanced vocabulary attempts to communicate, they are required to constantly "break things down," as in the former examples. This happens when a learner knows the meaning of a word in their native language but cannot translate it directly. Having to break down the meaning of words and phrases, like *intelligent*, *prima donna*, *high-maintenance*, and *inflated ego*, is an exercise in linguistic creativity. The learner, in other words, is forced to negotiate the meaning, and its expression, with words they have access to. This process crystallizes meaning and hones the skill of articulating a single thought or idea in multiple ways. When this process is repeated for hours on end, the result is a sharp linguistic mind with an enhanced creative faculty. This skill, of course, is one of general semantics, and is transferable to any language, including one's native language.

Those who know nothing of foreign languages know nothing of their own." (Johann Wolfgang von Goethe)[13]

I'm not saying that the best or most efficient way to improve one's native language skills is to study a foreign language. However, increased linguistic creativity is an inevitable byproduct of foreign language study. While there are other avenues through which foreign language study improves linguistic creativity, some more technical than others, the example I presented in this chapter stands out to me for its simplicity and for the frequency with which it occurs. For more on linguistic creativity, see chapter 16 on interpretation.

Chapter 8

The More Foreign Languages You Know, The Easier It Is To Learn New Ones

The hardest foreign language you will ever learn is your first one. And the second hardest foreign language you will ever learn is your second one. In other words, language learning gets easier with each subsequent iteration. This phenomenon owes to the fact that languages, especially those belonging to the same family, share a great deal in terms of grammar, syntax, phonetics, and vocabulary. If you've ever talked to a computer programmer, they will tell you the same thing. Having a background in one or two programming languages, especially if they are similar in structure and function, like Python and Java, makes it a lot easier to acquire new ones. Not only are many of the concepts repetitive across languages, but learners become more adept at recognizing patterns, formulating sentences, and memorizing information.

I'm still amazed whenever I encounter a bona fide polyglot, who can do more than order food and ask where the bathroom is. One polyglot who stands out to me is a history professor I had at Georgetown. Professor X spoke English, French, Spanish, Portuguese, Italian, Polish, and Japanese. He also read Chinese, Latin, and Ancient Greek. Professor X was raised multilingual; his family traveled a lot in his childhood, and he had dedicated a substantial part of his adult life to language-related pursuits. As far as I can tell, he is the best linguist, certainly in terms of breadth, I have ever met. A preponderance of effort inevitably went into acquiring–and maintaining–an inventory of language that vast. However, the process for Professor X most certainly got easier with each subsequent addition. For example, four of those languages–French, Spanish, Portuguese, and Italian–belong to the Romance language family. If it took 1,000 hours to learn the first one, then it would have taken a fraction of that time to learn the second, third, and fourth.

I happened to study Spanish, a Romance language, Arabic, a Semitic language, and Japanese, a Japonic language. These languages are about as different from one another as they come. Even so, there was a substantial amount of overlap that reduced the amount of time it took me to make headway. For example, Spanish and Arabic, unlike English, often omit subject pronouns and employ verb-first sentence constructs. In addition, both Spanish and Japanese have consistent pronunciation systems and quite similar-sounding vowels. Arabic and Japanese have elaborate ways to express the subjunctive and conditional moods, which took me a lot less time to learn with my background in Spanish. Spanish, for its part, was influenced by centuries of Arab rule, such that a number of Spanish words are derived from Arabic (many great differences between the two languages notwithstanding). Nonetheless, all the similarities referenced in this paragraph pale in comparison to those of the following example.

The Analogy Between French & Spanish

The summer of 2020 was my last semester at Ohio State before finishing my master's program in Middle East Studies. As part of the curriculum, I was required to enroll in French and German reading courses. The courses each consisted of 3 credits, and instruction took place remotely due to the outbreak of the pandemic. At that point, I had already opted not to pursue my PhD and knew I probably wouldn't have a context for reading French or German anytime soon. Moreover, like many other students around the world, I had mentally checked out due to global affairs and the virtual educational dynamic. The courses were assessed "pass" or "fail." My goal was to pass so I could graduate and move on with my life.

With that minimalist mindset, I was relieved to discover that French and Spanish grammar bore many striking resemblances, and it only took me minutes, rather than hours, to absorb many of the concepts. Similarities included gendered nouns and articles, formal and informal variants of the second person, parallel verb conjugations, including the subjunctive, multiple past tenses, and a boatload of cognates, among others. This experience opened my eyes to the principle outlined in the introduction to this chapter. I am now aware that this level of concordance is par for the course when dealing with languages of the same family. That said, French phonetics are notorious, and it takes a long time to get good at any language no matter how great the head start.

In sum, language is a transferable skill that can accelerate future learning, particularly in the domain of other languages belonging to the same family. While most people focus on a single second language, the number of people who have an interest in a third or fourth is not trivial. These types may be inspired to know that their potential to expand is enlarged.

Chapter 9

When Traveling, Country, Occupation,
and Lifestyle Influence Language
Learning Outcomes

Some people take it for granted that the fastest way to learn a foreign language is to travel or live in a country where it is spoken. The idea is that by being present in a cultured environment, the learner will dramatically grow their language skills, like water, sunlight, and Miracle Gro to a plant. Where else would the learner be more incentivized, if not socially obligated, to engage in their target language? This intuition, however, does not always square with reality. Language learning isn't formulaic, and the relationship between living in-country and language learning is easily overstated. Indeed, many people spend years in countries without progressing in the local language. When traveling, three main factors influence how much language improvement is likely to take place: 1) the destination country; 2) the traveler's occupation; and 3) the traveler's lifestyle.

Destination Country Influences Language Learning Outcomes

As a native English speaker, my language is spoken in many countries around the world. When I was in Jordan and Lebanon, there were signs in English posted everywhere, and most natives had some grasp of the language. A lot of natives viewed interactions with me as an opportunity to practice or show off their English. Similarly, if they detected that their English was better than my Arabic, they typically preferred to speak in my native language so we could have a better conversation. It follows that the educational and practical advantage of speaking English (or another common language) can lead to a conflict of interest for certain bilingual types.

Students of English as a foreign language, in contrast, get the full immersive experience in most American cities. This is because relatively few Americans are bilingual, and many bilingual Americans are eager to speak English since English is pervasive in American culture. Dare I say most learners who travel or study abroad in the US make great progress in the language.

Occupation Influences Language Learning Outcomes

The second factor–occupation–is critical because it dictates how travelers spend the lion's share of their time. Where target language practice is built into the occupational agenda, accelerated progress is the likely result. For example, on CLS Arabic (US State Department program) in Nizwa, Oman, during the summer of 2014, we had around four hours of Arabic class every day and numerous cultural activities with native speakers who were required to communicate with us in Arabic. As participants, we had to sign a language pledge only to speak Arabic amongst ourselves for two months (even though we all reneged). Middlebury College in Vermont, USA, is famous for similar immersion programs that expedite language development. The latter model consists of creating a linguistic-cultural enclave designed to simulate a native environment without the need for learners to geographically enter a target language country.

On the other hand, many people who live in a foreign country work a job in their native language. This phenomenon is even more common now with remote work surging in popularity. For example, I know several people who prefer to live in a non-English speaking country for cultural or environmental reasons, while earning a salary from a company that does business in English. It is not uncommon for people who work a job in their native language to make minimal progress in a target one. Obviously, this lack of learning depends on the time demands of a job and what the learner does in their free time, which leads me to my next point.

Lifestyle Influences Language Learning Outcomes

According to an article published by Comparitech, a cyber security and tech research company based in the UK, the average person worldwide spends around seven hours a day looking at a screen.[14] Realistically, an entrenched lifestyle habit like this is unlikely to change by sole virtue of being in a destination country. In fact, travelers may be inclined to document their experience and engage more with social media, or retreat from a new, strange environment into a known and comfortable corner of the internet. Aside from screentime, is the traveler frequently interacting with locals, on the town or in their homes, during their free time? Are these interactions being conducted in the traveler's native language or target language? There's a cliche in English, "You can take a horse to the water, but you can't make it drink." What we do where we are, particularly in the smartphone era, tends to be far more important than the location itself.

In sum, travel can be a great tool to foster linguistic and cultural immersion. Or it can amount to a wasted opportunity if we aren't intentional about applying ourselves. Allow me to illustrate.

My Japanese Got Worse in Japan

In the spring of 2015, I spent four months in Tokyo on a study abroad program through Sophia University, an affiliate college of Georgetown. What's ironic is that my Japanese regressed during that span. When you break it down, my experience fell short on all three of the factors—country, occupation, and lifestyle—that influence language learning outcomes abroad.

First, most people at Sophia University spoke good English. While this isn't true of everywhere in Japan, location within a country matters. I had friends who barely spoke any Japanese at all, and they got around just fine using their native or acquired English skills. While it would have been good practice for me to order food, navigate the metro, and converse with fellow students in Japanese, English typically sufficed for all these activities.

Second, Sophia University is an international college. English was the language of instruction for all my classes. You had to specially apply to take classes taught in Japanese. Naturally, few foreigners took these classes due to the high probability they would fail.

Third, my lifestyle wasn't conducive to language learning. Like my peers, I chose to socialize primarily with other internationals who shared my dormitory. Communication in Japanese was arduous, and there was no structured curriculum or social pressure prompting anyone to take the road less traveled. Often, my peers and I chose the more comfortable route of speaking English amongst ourselves.

Overall, I had a good time in Tokyo, and I hope to go back one day. I miss the people, the food, the cherry blossoms, the trains, the cityscapes, and the cutting-edge technology. Japan was full of imagination, and it's unlike any country I've ever visited. However, upon returning home, I decided to abandon Japanese in favor of Spanish and Arabic. I determined that the effort required to get good at Japanese paled in comparison to the scarce cultural and economic opportunities I was likely to receive in my future. My connection to Latin America and the Middle East was a lot stronger, and I already had my hands full with these languages and my other academic pursuits.

The Myth of Immersion

The myth of immersion isn't that immersion doesn't work. Immersion does work. The myth of immersion is that traveling to a foreign country is a necessary or sufficient step. People in the 21st century can experience the benefits of immersion wherever they are. They can consume target language media, change the language of their phones and search engines, find language partners using apps like HelloTalk, and practice translation throughout the day. What's more is that an immersive environment is only effective if the learner actively engages with it. I have been listening to birds chirp every morning for years, but I still have no idea what they're trying to communicate. As I mentioned in chapter 4, learning is not about what we see and hear, it's about what we are able to understand.

Chapter 10

Your Pronunciation Influences People's Perception of Your Language Skills

People do not have the time, resources, or interest to make informed judgments about everyone they meet and every situation they encounter. In the absence of better evidence, people rely on experience and external markers as a guide. If I see a white tiger roaming in my cul-de-sac, my brain is going to start releasing adrenaline, because of the general propensity of white tigers toward aggression. In reality, that white tiger may have escaped from the zoo. It may be sterilized. It may be a domestic pet with an unusually exotic exterior. Similarly, if we see someone with a muscular physique, we may make positive assumptions about their health and formidability, because a muscular physique has historically been associated with these qualities. Some of these assumptions may be deep-rooted, in cases where the external marker and its correlate exhibited a clear historical association. Let's say, for example, I discover that the white tiger in my cul-de-sac is a docile pet that escaped from its owner's home. Am I now suddenly going to interact with it like I would a golden retriever? I might or might not, depending on the strength of my conditioned bias. It's quite possible this deconditioning may take a long time, if I ever manage to dissociate the white tiger from danger.

Pronunciation as an External Marker of Language Ability

Pronunciation is an external marker of language ability with a strong historical association. People with the most accurate pronunciation per conventional norms (native speakers and experienced learners) are generally the ones who possess the most advanced language skills. Further qualifying pronunciation in this regard is the fact that it is one of the first things a listener notices about speech and is a recurrently observable feature of every utterance. In my experience, people often assess language ability based on how accurate the speaker's pronunciation is, in addition to other substantive markers of foreign language competence, like grammar, vocabulary, and style. I know people, for example, who get an exceptional amount of credit for their language ability due to their excellent pronunciation. I, on the other hand, observed that the opposite was true when I struggled to emulate a native Arabic pronunciation, despite my Jordanian roots. Logically, the need to rely on pronunciation as an external marker of language ability is most relevant during the initial stages of conversations. However, association between the two is an ongoing phenomenon.

Finally, accurate pronunciation facilitates clear communication and enables people to focus on the substance of a conversation rather than on its presentation. By the same token, the more accurate a speaker's pronunciation, the more comfortable they feel expressing themselves, and the greater their motivation is to engage. People with an interest in the practical or psycho-social benefits of an improved pronunciation may stand to gain from ideas presented in the following chapter.

Chapter 11

You Improve Your Pronunciation by Listening in the Target Language and Clearing Chronic Tension from the Voice

While learners invest a great deal of time in improving their grammar, vocabulary, and style to emulate native speech patterns, it is less common for them to do so with pronunciation, despite the myriad implications addressed in the previous chapter. Pronunciation is something that often gets taken for granted. Indeed, the ability to imitate non-native sounds and speech patterns is partly a function of genetics. Some people can put on a perfect foreign accent after minimal exposure to a target language, while others struggle with accurate pronunciation even after abundant exposure. It's the same reason why some people can sing, and others can't, no matter how much they practice.

The irony with pronunciation is that the ability to imitate sounds is virtually universal during the early years of childhood. For example, if you were raised by French or German parents, who spoke to you in their native language, then you would almost certainly speak with a native French or German pronunciation, regardless of your genetics or ethnicity. Comedian Wonho Chung is a case in point. Chung was born in Jeddah, Saudi Arabia to a South Korean father and Vietnamese mother and raised in Amman, Jordan. Chung speaks (and sings) in an Arabic that you would be hard-pressed to distinguish from his native counterparts. As people grow, they retain their ability to imitate sounds to varying degrees.

Pronunciation, like any other language skill, evolves with experience and can be improved with practice. My mother, for example, had a heavy Jordanian accent when she first moved to the US. She lamented the fact that people sometimes did not understand her, misunderstood her, or made unflattering assumptions about her intelligence based on her pronunciation. Decades later, my mother's pronunciation is more in line with conventional English norms, and her speech patterns evolved to match those of the speakers in her environment. The effect was subtle and gradual in live time, but the comparisons across decades of recordings reveal drastic changes. My mother's story stands out not for being unique, but because it illustrates a general point about the evolution of sound production. It is typical for a speaker's speech patterns to evolve after spending a significant amount of time in a country where the target language is spoken.

Listen Prolifically in the Target Language to Improve Your Pronunciation

The first step to imitate a sound is to develop a concept of it in the mind. For learners with their hearing faculty intact, listening is step one. There's a reason my high school Spanish teacher began every class for two weeks by orally reviewing consonant and vowel sounds. Pronouncing words in a foreign language as we would words in our native language is the fastest way to butcher an accent. In fact, beginning to speak a foreign language without studying pronunciation can lead to bad phonetic habits that may take time to unlearn down the road.

In the same way, we often retain the speech patterns of our first language professors. For example, someone who was taught English by a Briton, American, or Indian professor with a heavy accent, may retain pronunciation patterns characteristic of that individual. I know of language curriculums that do not incorporate speaking for several weeks or months partially so that learners can first develop a deeper concept of a language's sound. In any case, the more we listen intently, and pay careful attention to new sounds, the greater the probability we will be able to produce an accurate pronunciation.

Certain pronunciation challenges are generalizable across populations. For example, native English speakers may struggle to articulate the Spanish R; French R and French U; German R; and the Arabic Qaaf, Ayn, Ha, Hamza, and Ghayn sounds. On the other hand, the English letters B, R, L, S, V, W, and Z, as well as numerous other sounds, like "th," and "ed," may pose challenges to non-native English speakers, depending on their mother tongue. In addition to learning new sounds that are non-existent or uncommon in one's native language, mastering old, familiar sounds in the context of a target language takes time. In sum, the more we listen to our target language and imitate the speech patterns of native speakers, the faster we will reach our peak phonetic potential.

Get Rid of Vocal Tension to Improve Your Pronunciation

Pronunciation is also a function of tension in the voice, which is a dynamic factor. People who carry tension in their voice are less nimble when speaking, singing, and imitating sounds. Therefore, tension is routinely referred to as "the enemy of the singer" (let alone the ventriloquist), and you can find countless exercises on YouTube aimed at reducing vocal tension (lip roll, tongue trill, straw phonation, etc.). After doing vocal exercises or consuming substances that relax the muscles in the throat, people who carry tension in their voice often notice a marked improvement in their ability to speak clearly and flexibly, which can translate to a more accurate pronunciation.

Tension is a kind of stress that gets attached to an organism. It is a holistic marker that can be triggered or exacerbated by anxiety, unresolved emotional issues, and poor dietary and lifestyle choices. Tension may be chronic and stable as an ongoing condition, or it may be acute and transitory, appearing only at certain times in response to environmental or psychological triggers. Relieving vocal tension starts by identifying its chronic and acute causes, and taking steps to mitigate them. In addition, many people find relief by performing vocal exercises in advance of a performance or speaking session, or as a general preventative/therapeutic measure. Vocal therapists, for example, routinely prescribe straw phonation and other anal-ogous exercises to relieve tension and restore full functioning of the voice.

How I Learned to Pronounce the Spanish R

In high school, it used to drive me crazy that I couldn't pronounce the Spanish R. Being able to pronounce the Spanish R was like a badge of honor that all serious learners of Spanish were expected to wear. The sound is a lot more subtle than the exaggerated caricature that people commonly conceive of. However, this didn't stop me from going above and beyond to achieve my goal. I got on YouTube (Yes, YouTube was a thing in 2010) and watched several videos of people teaching gringos how to pronounce the Spanish R. I remember one guy said put your tongue on the hard palate above your two front teeth and make a sound. That was pretty much my strategy for the next several weeks. I remember going around the neighborhood marketing my brother's painting business, while making incoherent fluttering sounds in between stops. I also did this in Spanish class, a lot less fre-quently, but still enough to garner a reputation.

It must have been three or four weeks before I articulated my first Spanish R, and a few weeks after that before it became a smooth utterance.

My friends still remind me more than a decade later how annoying my Spanish R obsession was. However, given that I still enjoy doing vocal trills to this day, I would say that I'm the one who got the last laugh.

Chapter 12

Learning A Foreign Language May Change Your Personality

"One who speaks only one language is one person, but one who speaks two languages is two people." (Turkish Proverb)[15]

In chapter two, I addressed the salient decline in communication skills and expressive power that characterizes the early stages of foreign language acquisition. However, the effect of learning a foreign language on personality is not all regressive. Just as foreign language study temporarily disables certain personality traits, it also affords the opportunity to create, reinvent, and redefine other ones.

The Hysteria of Arabic 101

I recall the hysterical atmosphere of one of my college Arabic classes taught by a teaching assistant (TA). The smallest, most mundane utterances in Arabic would trigger laughter and jokes for which there was no parallel in English. Somehow, Arabic and comedy became inseparable, and everybody was acting buzzed all the time. I suppose the bar for comedy was a lot lower. It is easy for native speakers to become desensitized to poetry, humor, and other artistic forms to which they are routinely exposed. On the other hand, there was an element of unpredictability. Since we were intermediate learners and did not possess a strong situational command of the language, our utterances were fool's gold layered on top of fool's gold. This was especially true during improvised skits and conversations where we had to get creative to keep things moving.

Systemic-level factors aside, I think the most decisive factor in the equation was the attitude my teacher brought to the language. Arabic, for that TA, was fun. She reportedly had a blast in rural Jordan for years before transitioning into academia. Her light-hearted disposition toward the language was reflected in the classroom environment she cultivated and infected everybody like a contagion.

The "Joy of No Expectations"

Most of the language classes I've taken were not hysterical, and that's probably a good thing. However, I have observed that some people feel more comfortable expressing certain aspects of their personality in a non-native language. Even though it is technically more difficult to do so, there are often fewer social and psychological barriers. Call this "the joy of low expectations." Or, just as well, "the joy of no expectations," in terms of how people are supposed to present themselves in public. In a learner's native language, there are expectations about what they are going to say and how they are going to act based on memories of past behavior. When they deviate from those norms, they are often met with friction. (*Why is this person saying this or acting that way? This just doesn't feel right.*) As I addressed in chapter 10, the mind seeks to make sense of the world, so it can predict future events and adapt itself accordingly. Upsets to paradigms take time for people to process, and their most immediate response is typically one of resistance. This dynamic has the effect of re-inforcing behavioral norms, both in oneself and others.

In a foreign language, a lot of social and psychological conditioning gets thrown out the window. First, you begin to interact with people who do not know you outside of the target language. The blank canvas effect here is true of any new people you meet in general. Second, every language is a world unto itself. It is common to hear people comment on the particularity of an individual's foreign language skills. *She speaks French well. His Spanish is formal or funny. I want to hear them speak Arabic.* In other words, people expect there to be some differences between the native-language version of yourself and the target-language version. If you want to exaggerate these differences, then more power to you. As the saying in the intro goes, the multiple personalities effect with people who speak more than one language is real but bears none of the oft associated pathology.

I kept a journal in Spanish as a freshman and sophomore at Georgetown. Spanish gave me a vehicle to write about things that I might have hesitated to commit to paper in my native language. Maybe it was a sense of privacy. Few of the people I hung out with at Georgetown spoke Spanish. It wasn't that I wrote about anything super sensitive, but Spanish enabled me to carve out a private headspace where everything was confidential (at least theoretically). Confidentiality, in fact, was one of my initial motivations for learning Spanish. I used to pass notes in high school with my Puerto Rican friend, Kevin, back in the day when teachers didn't let kids talk in class.

In sum, language skills and personality are interrelated, and personality is often governed by social and psychological expectations. The widening or removal of expectations, under the right circumstances, can afford greater freedom of expression in a foreign language, even if the technical process of communication itself is more difficult.

Chapter 13

Learning A Foreign Language May Make You Less Popular

It's hard to connect with someone if you don't speak their language. With that understanding, this chapter heading doesn't make a lot of intuitive sense. Indeed, language skills enable relationships that would otherwise be impossible. They are a cultural asset, if not a downright social and economic necessity. However, it is the *exception* to the rule that I want to expand on in this heading. It applies mainly to people whose native language is English, or another language popular among a host community.

I read a provocative article a few years ago published in Japan Today whose main point had a lot of truth to it.[16] The author, who spent "at least 4,000 hours actively studying [Japanese]"–not counting entertainment, media, work, and daily conversations–observed that many of the locals preferred to speak English with him, no matter how eloquent he waxed in their native language. Writing hyperbolically, he explained, "Your magic trick is that you can speak English. That's what everyone wants you

71

to do." He noted that most foreigners did just fine without speaking the language, and that "Contrary to many countries that demand you speak the local language, Japan sometimes seems to prefer you don't speak Japanese."

That is one man's experience living at a particular place in a particular country at a particular time. It doesn't speak for all people studying Japanese, and it certainly does not speak for all people studying foreign languages. However, as I alluded to in chapter 9 on travel, many people I encountered in Japan and the Middle East were eager to practice, or show off, their English skills with a native speaker. One of my good friends from coastal Colombia, for whom English is like the holy grail, embodies this mindset to the tee. Even though his Spanish is excellent, he can't be bothered to speak it with native English speakers.

Another critical factor in the equation is language level. While the author of the article reports being highly advanced in Japanese, I'd venture to say that most people who study Japanese, and other "critical languages," are not. On the other hand, it is common to find people in various parts of the world who are highly proficient in English due to its prevalence in the business world and global status as a lingua franca. I recall, for example, that one of my uncles in Jordan would always respond to me in English. His English was better than my Arabic, which meant that it was easier for us to communicate in English, and that is what we often did. ("The rich get richer.") So, in addition to social, cultural, and economic considerations, proficiency is another variable that factors into the equation of what language people prefer to speak.

To be sure, it is likely that many people you interact with will not speak your native language well or have an interest in learning it. (With English, I have observed this to be true in large parts of Japan, the Middle East, and Latin America.) In these cases, proficiency in their native language is an unqualified social advantage. In sum, the general wisdom that foreign language skills facilitate human connections and open doors of economic and cultural opportunity is highly dependable. It's pertinent to keep in mind, however, that not everyone you interact with will be eager to communicate with you in their native language.

Chapter 14

Language Immersion in the 21st Century Is Possible Wherever You Are

Conventional wisdom has it that the best way to learn a foreign language is via immersion. The term *language immersion* generally denotes the experience of being in an environment where a target language is ubiquitous (Germany and German, for example). It may also have a more particular application, such as classroom instruction, classroom interactions, or a language program that simulates a native environment. Practice, as they say, makes perfect. The expectation is that learners in an immersive environment will read, write, speak, and listen in a target language more than they would otherwise. Native speakers, the gold standard of language proficiency, are immersed in their native language for hours every day, from morning to night, for years on end, which is why it is second nature.

Historically, travel and language immersion programs were the best, if not only, way to achieve language immersion. If you wanted to be immersed in German or Swahili in the 1950s, you had to physically be around people who spoke the language. In chapter 9, I addressed three factors—country, occupation, and life-style—that dictate the extent to which travel can facilitate language immersion. On the other hand, language immersion programs (CLS, Middlebury, or something more local) generally do an excellent job of this since they are designed with the express goal of language improvement. That said, travel and language immersion programs aren't available to everyone, and certainly not to everyone at all times of the year.

Technology has radically transformed the landscape of language learning, and the bulk of that change has transpired in the last two decades. IBM released the first smartphone in 1994, and it took several years for Blackberry, followed by iPhone and Android devices, to gain mainstream status. Today, it is uncommon to meet someone in the US who doesn't possess a smartphone. The same is true of people in many other countries, and increasingly so in places historically less developed. As smartphone technology becomes more necessary in a world powered by mobile applications, this trend is only going to continue.

Today, if I want to immerse myself in German or Swahili, I don't need to know anyone in-person who speaks those languages (although that would be helpful). What I need is YouTube to watch instructional videos and consume native content in those languages. I need Linguee, MobiTUKI, and other online dictionaries complete with robust example sentences. I need HelloTalk, Italki, WhatsApp, Reddit, and other platforms that unite teachers, students, and fellow language learners. Today, it's easier than ever to get a language question about grammar, vocabulary, slang, or local usage addressed. And it's similarly easier than ever to find instructors, language buddies, and native content in a target language that can make for an in-person or virtually immersive environment.

Habits of Daily Language Immersion

Language skills, like muscles, need to be regularly exercised to maintain peak performance. Good linguists will spend a few hours every week, if not every day, working with each of their target languages, independent of environmental dictates. As someone who's been studying languages for 14+ years, I've only taken classes for maybe a third of that time. To stay immersed year-round, I start with the "low-hanging fruit." If there's a sporting event, like an

NBA, NFL, or World Cup game that I'm already going to be watching in English, I check to see if there is an alternative broadcast with Spanish-speaking commentators. (In the US, Spanish-language programming is widely accessible.) If I'm watching a Netflix program in English, I have a habit of putting Spanish or Arabic subtitles on. (Even in a group setting, most people don't mind.) By the same token, it's rare to catch me driving without some target language music, podcast or YouTube program playing in the background.

I inevitably come across new words all the time. For Spanish, I like to consult SpanishDict.com for quick word lookups; Tureng.com for slang; and HelloTalk and Reddit community forums for more localisms. If I want to consult further, I will message a Spanish-speaking friend on WhatsApp. I have a similar process for Arabic, where I like to consult Aratools.com for quick word lookups and Lughatuna for slang. Linguee is another great dictionary and reference with example sentences that currently supports Spanish, French, German, Italian, Chinese, Russian, Japanese, Portuguese, and Dutch.

A half hour here, an hour there, and fifteen minutes sprinkled in throughout the day make a big difference in terms of language acquisition and language maintenance. Small daily exposure is especially critical during "off-peak" seasons when the learner is not regularly engaging in the target language. During this time, the learner may want to make modest progress or, at the very least, keep their skills from deteriorating. For three "atomic" habits that work wonders in this regard, see chapters 15, 16, and 17.

Chapter 15

Atomic Habit #1: Thinking in the Target Language

The human brain is constantly generating thoughts, and many of those thoughts consist of words. If you Google "How many thoughts do we think in a day?" you will be met with a wide range of estimates. One common estimate attributed to the National Science Foundation that has been circulating online for years is 12,000 to 60,000. The figure 70,000 has gotten similar press despite the absence of an authenticable source. However, recent research has come away with more modest conclusions. A 2020 study done by a team of researchers at Queen's University in Canada using brain image scans that tracked the number of thought transitions (or new "thought worms") found that the figure was closer to 6,000 per day, not including sleeping time (6,240, if you factor in 8 hours of sleep per night).[17] The researchers also found an association between personality traits and thought transition rate, whereby participants high in "openness" yielded a lower thought transition rate, and participants high in "neuroticism" yielded a higher one.

Even this lower new data amounts to a grand average of more than six thoughts per minute, or a thought every ten seconds, which, to my mind, is an incredibly high number. There's a reason almost all humans are proficient in at least one language. With that much action in between the ears comes a lot of opportunities to improve language skills. Our brains have evolved to utilize language at a prolific rate, both as passive recipients of communication and as active creators of our own. It is said that most of our thoughts are repetitive.[18] They're either similar or identical to thoughts we've had in the past, whether that's yesterday, last week, or just moments ago. The question is do we want to invest all the verbal currency of our *mundane* thought life into our native language, where it is largely a repetitive cycle with little progressive potential, or in a target language, whose potential is vast?

Thinking is something we are already doing all the time. As linguists and language learners, we can channel our brain's verbal activity to improve or maintain our language skills, without making any major modifications to our lifestyle or environment. The language we think in throughout the day becomes second nature; our level of comfort, ease, and fluency dramatically increase over time. Thinking in a foreign language is destined to be laborious at first. Beginners and intermediate learners will have trouble formulating coherent thoughts in a timely fashion. However, in the weeks and months that follow, new initiates are likely to find, as I did, that the process becomes more fluid and enjoyable. What started out difficult, like running, will wind up being easy, like breathing, even if it takes months or years to make that progression.

Being able to passively understand a word in speech or writing is different from being able to actively use that word in context. The transition from "passive vocabulary" to "active vocabulary" comes with experience. Thinking (and speaking and writing) in a language is the surest way to accelerate this process. Not only do these productive activities help us grow and sharpen our active vocabulary, but they can also serve as a prompt for further learning. For example, when we actively engage with the target language in this fashion, we will be able to identify new words that are unknown to us, or old words, whose full range of meaning is not entirely clear. These "blocks" in the process present an opportunity to expand our knowledge, as we exercise reason and consult dictionaries and references as needed. Given that our thoughts typically pertain to lived experience, the outcome is a more practically relevant skill set.

Don't Venture Too Far Off Base

My Iraqi Arabic professor in college always used to say, "Stick to what you know." What she meant was, if we were not clear about the meaning or usage of a word or grammatical item, it was better to opt for a more familiar one when speaking or writing. The reasoning, as I understand, was twofold. One, when we liberally use unfamiliar words and constructs, we are likely to make a lot of mistakes and reinforce bad habits, especially where no mechanism of accountability is present. In my observation, most mistakes language students make in the classroom go uncorrected (at least in speaking, if not in writing). And almost all a learner's errors in the "real world" go uncorrected. Not everyone is inclined to correct speech, particularly if what the other person is saying can be understood, and not all people take kindly to being corrected. The bottom line is that if we are loose with our language habits, if we don't routinely inquire into areas of doubt or uncertainty, there will be a lot of unlearning and relearning in our future.

Advanced learners are likely to profit from, and enjoy, thinking in a target language the most. Even if beginner and intermediate students follow the advice of the previous paragraph, a limited language base may make the process feel disjointed and tedious. However, the same is true of other productive activities, i.e., speaking and writing. Thoughts are a precursor and prerequisite of speaking and writing and have similar implications. If one is going to limit a single productive activity in the interest of acquiring a greater language base, then it may make sense to limit them all. All in all, striking a balance between language "input" (listening and reading) and language "output" (thinking, speaking, and writing) is the winning formula for most language learners of all levels.

Lifestyle of a Linguist

The best linguists don't let their skills fall by the wayside just because class let out and they don't currently have anyone from the target language community to communicate with on a regular basis. During times when our environment is not conducive to language learning, the habit of thinking in a target language may be especially helpful in efforts to maintain or improve language skills. I know it has helped me as a professional linguist, multilingual, and hobbyist do exactly that when life would otherwise have gotten in the way.

When I initially shared the main point of this section on Reddit (r/languagelearning), I was taken aback by the lively response. (The post garnered ~1,000 likes, ~100 comments, and ~10 trophies.) It was a simple idea that resonated with many language learners and had evidently occurred only to few. Today, when doing routine "accountability" checks with some of my language buddies, it is common for me to ask them, "Have you been thinking in English?"

Chapter 16

Atomic Habit #2: Interpretation in the Target Language

Life comes with a lot of fluff mixed in. No organization, institution, or process is perfectly efficient, and even those that excel by this metric are not perfectly tailored to the needs of everyone. I can't tell you how many hours I've spent in lectures and meetings that did not add a whole lot of value to my life. Even though I needed to be present for a variety of reasons, I did not need to internalize every word that was spoken. How can a language learner make the most of their time under such circumstances? Enter the habit of interpretation. Interpretation, of course, can be practiced all the time, not just during downtime.

Interpretation, unlike translation, which is a more catch-all term, entails speech being uttered in real time. When I was in college, I made a habit of translating segments of speech or entire lectures into Spanish or Arabic (in my head, of course), depending on my interest level and the relevance of the material. I would also do this while watching sports or TV in my native language. I told myself, "If I'm going to be watching sports or TV in English, I need to be doing something productive." While a sport like American football, with frequent intermissions, was ideal for vocabulary and memorization activities, interpretation could be done in any spoken word context. Interpretation challenged me to think creatively in my target languages. It prompted the acquisition of new language knowledge and increased the speed with which I could formulate coherent thoughts.

I've organized the rest of this section into a series of "pro tips" that stem from many hundreds of hours practicing interpretation over the years in a wide variety of contexts. To be sure, the habit of interpretation is best reserved for intermediate to advanced learners. It is an even more advanced skill than "thinking in a foreign language," because the interpreter, unlike the thinker, has no control over the narrative. Once a learner has a solid foundation of grammar and an ample vocabulary in their target language, then they can begin to put this skill into practice.

Pro Tip #1: Start with the Simple and the Familiar

If you do not have a background in the genre or register of language being used, there will likely be large gaps in interpretation. Depending on your level, you may struggle to find any kind of rhythm whatsoever. As a result, it is advisable to start with the simplest spoken material you have access to. For example, a rabid sports fan may identify that a sports broadcast, with a fixed context, a predictable plot, large pauses, and numerous proper nouns is a good place to start. In addition, you won't want to interpret in settings that you really need to be present for, e.g., a review session for your organic chemistry final or your boss's presentation of annual performance reviews. Until interpretation becomes second nature, there will be a substantial drop-off in retention, even as one's language skills develop.

Pro Tip #2: Break Down Unknown Words

In cases where you do not know how to directly translate what's being said, you will need to "break it down." For example, if I can't recall how to translate *library*, I may instead render it as *a place where books are housed for the public*, or instead of *gym*, I may render it as *a place with equipment where people go to work out*. "Breaking it down" is a skill that you will get good at over time. It will make you a better interpreter, improve your linguistic creativity, and grow your working knowledge of semantics.

Pro Tip #3: Befriend the Dictionary

Interpretation will expose gaps in your language ability. Gaps consisting of words, expressions, idioms, and grammar. Whenever you have a doubt, get out your dictionary. ("When in doubt, get it out.") If you want to maintain some semblance of flow or don't have immediate access to a dictionary, you can take notes of the words and expressions you need to look up. As you gain experience, the number of items you stand to gain from looking up will decrease. If dictionary fatigue or burnout begins to set in, then you can spend less time on looking things up and more time on mastering what you already know. As I addressed in chapter #5 on avoiding burnout, you don't want to wear yourself down psychologically or emotionally.

Pro Tip #4: All Roads Lead to Rome

A good interpreter is someone who can consistently and accurately produce a translation in live time. What this means is that the translation does not have to be perfect. You may not be able to render every metaphor and idiom as such within a moment's notice, but you eventually need to be able to generate quick translations that capture the *meaning* of what is being said. In every language, there are countless ways to communicate the same idea. Interpretation, it follows, is an exercise in linguistic creativity.

Pro Tip #5: Watch Movies with Subtitles and Compare the Transcripts

Most streaming services, including Netflix, Amazon Prime Video, and Disney+, offer subtitles in a variety of languages. It is instructive to see how experts who get paid big bucks move material from one language to another. It is also possible to download bilingual subtitles from the internet and select streaming platforms. Having bilingual transcripts on hand makes it easier to skip around, draw comparisons, and study the language. While the mantra "speed kills" epitomizes interpretation like none other, slowing things down using the written word as an aid can facilitate this objective. Athletes, dancers, performers, public speakers, and musicians have a reputation for doing the same. Once the fundamentals of an art have been mastered, then speeding things up is only a matter of repetition.

Persistence Is the Name of the Game

Interpretation is no walk in the park, especially "simultaneous interpretation," where there are no breaks in the action. (Simultaneous interpreters typically work remotely, whereas consecutive interpreters are employed at bilingual events and alternate with the speaker in between utterances.) Interpretation is also not for everybody, regardless of their language level. I know career linguists who won't interpret because it's just not their specialty. However, there are a host of benefits that accompany the discipline, whether someone takes up work as an interpreter or not. These benefits include increased linguistic creativity, a greater knowledge of semantics, and the ability to produce accurate speech on the fly. Like thinking in a foreign language, interpretation is a skill most of us can practice daily without altering our lifestyle or making any special time provision.

Chapter 17

Atomic Habit #3: Leveraging Screentime in the Target Language

In chapter 9, I cited research findings that the average person worldwide spends around seven hours a day looking at a screen, most of which time is on a mobile device. When the iOS Screen Time function came out in 2018, which gives the user a detailed breakdown of their mobile usage, it was a moment of truth for the world. Many people were alarmed to discover how much total time they spent staring at their mobile device– and where that time was going.

Language learners can start to get more out of their screentime by changing the default language of their phones. The default language impacts titles, descriptions, and the text that appears on the native interface and in various applications. This change can be part of a broader strategy to sustain language immersion year-round. While advanced students stand to gain the most from atomic habit #3, beginners and intermediates can begin to experiment with the ideas I present below.

Surfing the Web as a Linguistic Exercise

For most of human history, people were dependent on their parents, teachers, and in-person relationships to learn about various subjects. It wasn't for centuries after the printing press was invented in the mid-15th century that mass literacy became common in many parts of the world, and even longer before it was common to have a library of books and information at one's disposal. The invention of the internet was a seminal event in human history. Over time, the extent and quality of information available on the world wide web has improved dramatically. When you take an intellectually curious person and equip them with a smartphone and internet access, there's no telling how many hours a day they will spend absorbed in cyberspace. I recall being a prolific user of Google since high school and attribute much of what I have learned to my habit of looking things up.

Recently, I had an epiphany relating to screentime. I realized that one, I was spending a few hours a day on average browsing online; two, not all these activities needed to be conducted in English; and three, I could streamline some of my goals by allocating a portion of that time to my target language. Now, for example, instead of consuming articles exclusively in English, I will conduct many searches in Spanish or Arabic. iOS has a built-in feature where you can highlight a word and access the definition or translation in your desired language. While Android does not have a built-in dictionary, there are a handful of apps that perform the same function.

Using Google's Autocomplete Predictions to Stimulate Curiosity

Google has a cool "autocomplete" function that presents you with a list of popular keywords and phrases as you enter text in the search bar. For example, if I enter "How to go," several suggestions appear beginning with that phrase, including "live on tiktok" "back in time on google earth," and "to sleep fast." As I modify the text, these suggestions update in live time, and I can choose to click on them or continue with my custom search. Autocomplete has the dual benefit of one, exposing a language learner to popular language samples in a target language. The language learner can read hundreds, if not thousands of sample searches within minutes. And two, autocomplete can connect the language learner with stimulating content to consume.

To be sure, I don't always conduct my searches in a target language. English is the most popular language online and the preferred medium of many publishers and content creators. I may also opt for English if my search parameter is technical, if I want a quick answer to a question, or if I identify a decline in the quality of search results in my target language. However, I now search in my target language enough of the time that it constitutes a substantial change to my routines.

In sum, Chapters 15-17 have demonstrated the extent to which language is ubiquitous in our daily lives. So much of what we do from morning to night involves words in one fashion or another. By thinking in a foreign language, practicing interpretation, and implementing some of the ideas mentioned in this paragraph, we can maximize our time in the interest of language learning without radically altering our lifestyle.

Chapter 18

Embrace Being Corrected as a Means of Progress

Fear of making mistakes is an enemy of learning. It is often motivated by the desire to protect one's reputation or identity. We don't want to make mistakes due to what others might think, or how it might conflict with our self-image. However, an ego that needs protection in this fashion is a facade. It's not based in reality; therefore, it isn't sustainable. If that weren't bad enough, it deprives the learner of opportunities to experiment and grow. Whereas ego wants to be celebrated for what it already knows and fears the unknown, intellectual curiosity is constantly seeking to expand its knowledge.

They say we learn the most, not from the things we get right, but from the things we get wrong. I have certainly found that to be true on my language learning journey. Positive reinforcement is important for psychological reasons, and it inspires us to "keep doing what we're doing." However, correction promises more in terms of objective progress. It is, in fact,

95

one of the biggest things you are paying for with an education. Anyone can watch lectures online and take notes, but personal feedback is the thing most relevant for individual progress.

Correction is hard work. However, when teachers, friends, and language buddies detect that we are receptive to correction, they are more likely to offer it. In addition, an intellectually curious mindset, in general, inspires people to share their knowledge. "You can also say. . ." Or "My personal favorite is. . ." Or "We have an expression for that. . ." I've learned a ton from online dictionaries and references. Certainly, the need to ask people how to define words and use them in context is a lot less pressing than it was before this technology was available. However, I have found that my retention tends to be greater when I learn something from another human being. The context is more personal, the memory is more vivid, and the recall is sharper. And it's a two-way line of communication, so I can direct follow-up questions as needed. Even if someone corrects us with dubious intentions, we always stand to gain something in the process.

Your Language Notes, Graded Papers, and Chat History Are a Resource

I'm a minimalist. I don't hang on to too much stuff from my past, whether it's material or digital. I had an old iPhone 6s that was 16 GB back when Apple made phones with that little storage, and I remember constantly having to delete data to free up space. However, among the things I never deleted were my target language histories on iMessage and WhatsApp. It's amusing to go back and read these from time to time. It's also constructive from a linguistic standpoint. I used to ask people to correct me, and they often did. I would review their corrections from time to time and refresh myself on the language contained in those exchanges. In addition, periodically reviewing old exchanges can elucidate our progress. Just as bodybuilders take before-and-after photos to motivate and inspire, linguists can do the same with their language samples. Sometimes it's easy to get so caught up in where we want to be that we fail to appreciate how far we've come.

Similarly, I have notes on my phone full of vocabulary, expressions, and grammar that I periodically revisit. I haven't been in school for a while, but I used to do the same with my graded papers. Corrections (and remedial notes) are a resource. They require effort from someone else (or ourselves), and I personally don't want that effort to go to waste. Mistakes are an opportunity to get better, but there's no sense in making the same one multiple times, hence the value of repetition.

You know the old adage, "Sweat in training so you don't bleed in war." As melodramatic as it is in the context of education, there's an analogy to be made. The stakes of messing up around friends, teachers, and language buddies are relatively low. The more mistakes we process in this environment, the fewer will be left to make when the stakes are relatively high. For my part, I'd rather a mistake cost me a small bit of ego now than a business or cultural opportunity down the road.

Chapter 19

Progress in a Foreign Language Should Be Measured in Hours, Not Months or Years

If you ask someone how long they've been studying a foreign language, chances are they're going to respond in units of months or years. "6 months." "2 years." "A decade." A super precise figure is rarely ever in demand, so this language is preferable in most contexts. However, the only relevant unit of measure in terms of language learning is hours. In a school system or program, with a structured curriculum, the larger metrics equate to a fixed number of hours of classroom instruction. For example, to progress through level one of Swahili, one may be required to complete 100 hours of classroom instruction. However, the levels say nothing about how much time the learner spends doing homework and engaging with the language outside of class. Once formal education is complete, the units of months and years are even less relevant. In a word, there's a reason why all the averages presented in chapter one on how long it takes to become proficient in a foreign language are measured in hours. Hours quantify application, whereas large increments like months and years say little, if anything, about how much total time was dedicated to learning.

Today, I can tell you how many years I've been studying my target languages. However, if you asked me how many hours I've been studying them, my answer would be "I don't know." I could certainly approximate and provide a general range, but that's not the point. The point is when we measure our progress, we should be thinking in terms of application. "How many *hours* do I need to put in to get where I want to be in the next x months or years?" This practical shift can keep expectations more in line with reality. It protects against disappointment (*Why am I not a master of Chinese after taking classes for 4 years?*); and it can inform the lifestyle and study habits we develop in pursuit of our goals.

Accelerating Time in Pursuit of Language Proficiency

In chapters 2 and 9, I referenced my experience in Nizwa, Oman, during the summer of 2015, studying Arabic intensively on a critical language scholarship. The program was structured such that we had around five hours of Arabic language instruction every day, including cultural activities, let alone homework, free time, and socialization. Two months in this environment was considered the equivalent of one year of normal classroom instruction. Oral proficiency interviews (OPIs) were administered at the beginning and end of the program. I remember going from Advanced Low (7/10), having taken formal Arabic at Georgetown for two years, to Advanced Mid (8/10) by the end of the summer. It was typical of students on the program to jump at least one level. It follows that if someone were able to sustain an intensive environment like this for an entire year, that year might amount to the equivalent of *six* years of normal classroom instruction.

In retrospect, there were weeks and months where I might easily average 5+ solid hours of application a day in my target language. Maybe I was preparing to take an exam, working a job, or, for whatever reason, feeling especially motivated. Similarly, there were weeks and months where I scarcely applied myself at all and my language skills regressed. Don't think in months or years. Think in hours.

Chapter 20

Linguistic "Muscle Memory" Is A Real Thing

In the early stages of word processing technology, the AutoSave function had yet to be implemented. This meant you had to manually press the "save" button periodically or run the risk of losing everything you had been working on up until that point. It wasn't uncommon for a computer to freeze or a user to forget to press save before x-ing out of the document. Disastrous. I venture to say that almost every millennial and most Gen Zers have at least one horror story featuring their hard digital work going down the drain. Today, AutoSave is standard on major word processors, like Microsoft Word and Google Docs. Hard work is costly, and people who work hard have an interest in safeguarding it. Insurance, security systems, and cloud computing are all designed with this goal in mind.

The term *muscle memory* refers to the brain's ability to develop a new skill through practice. The classical example is learning to ride a bike. At first, the process is rough; you fall and scrape your knee multiple times. With each session, however, you gain a little more motor coordination, and your baseline for the next session improves. Eventually, you acquire enough muscle memory where you can ride a bike smoothly and effortlessly. The same concept applies to sports, dance, music, art, cooking, martial arts, etc., where learning, or "memory," takes place via repetition.

That said, what happens when you take a long break without engaging in any of these activities—say weeks, months, or even years? Muscle memory, in popular discourse, refers to the phenomenon whereby people can *relearn* old skills much faster than the time it initially took them to acquire them. For example, you go five years without riding your bike. When you first start up again, it's rough, like it was before you initially learned. You scrape your knee a few times. However, within a few hours, you're back at the level where you left off, coasting smoothly in the neighborhood. Muscle memory is a term that commonly gets brought up in the context of bodybuilding. Who would want to work hard for years to build muscle mass, only to lose it within a few months of inactivity, and then need to work just as hard for the same length of time to get it back? However, pretty much any athlete will tell you that it's a lot easier to put the muscle back on the second time around.

New research is attempting to better understand muscle memory and there are different theories based on its various applications. You can look that up on your own time, as I am not the most qualified person to present it. However, what I am going to do is add my drop to the bucket of anecdotal evidence on the topic, as it relates to language learning. The idea that you can relearn knowledge faster and more efficiently than the first time you learned it is not revolutionary. However, one day it may become relevant for people who have invested a lot of time in their language skills.

"Muscle Memory" and Language Learning

I try to keep my Spanish and Arabic fresh year-round, regardless of my current academic, professional, geographic, or personal situation. However, I have not always been able to execute on this goal. I've gone weeks, and even months, without doing much at all in either of these languages. I've found that uncommon vocabulary is the first thing to go, which is intuitive. Uncommon vocabulary gets the least amount of reinforcement to begin with, and so the learner's command of it is relatively less strong. However, I don't recall ever having an issue with major grammar concepts. This also makes intuitive sense since grammar is something that gets re-inforced all the time. While I may see a less common word once a week or even once a month, most grammar gets utilized on a daily or weekly basis. (One notable exception for me was the case endings of written Arabic. These case endings have some elaborate rules that occasionally need reviewed, but the grammar retention principle applies to spoken Arabic.)

I've heard bodybuilders speak in terms of a "mature muscle." This isn't a scientific term, but what they are talking about is the muscle that sticks around longer–or doesn't go away at all–when they stop working out for a period. I liken this to grammar and active vocabulary that is deeply ingrained in our minds. Naturally, we don't forget them as easily. And, if we do forget them, they take us the least amount of time to relearn. I recall flipping through my Japanese textbooks several years removed from any activity in the language. While I had effectively forgotten most of what I had learned, the grammar concepts and vocabulary that I once knew quite well seemed relatively easy to reacquire. At that moment, I knew that if I ever wanted to take up Japanese again, I would have a much easier time regaining my old level. Similarly, I have found that periodically reviewing old forgotten grammar notes, vocabulary, and idioms in my target languages requires less effort.

Speak Arabic to Me, Binyamin!

I have a friend from my graduate school days at The Ohio State University whom we nicknamed Aladdin. Aladdin and I took a number of Arabic classes together. Every now and then, we would play pick-up basketball at the university gym. Aladdin couldn't shoot, but he was one of the quickest, most intense defenders I have ever seen. One day, he went high up for a layup at 100 mph, bumped a defender, and fell square on his head. Aladdin lay there motionless for a few minutes before gingerly getting up. He had apparently suffered a concussion. We drove him to the ER, before he decided in the reception that he felt okay enough to go home. I'll never forget, while we were leaving the gym and during the car ride, Aladdin kept asking people to speak Arabic to him. I probably heard the phrase "Speak Arabic to me, Binyamin! [my Arabic name]" at least two dozen times. Aladdin, in his dizzied and confused state, waiting to be seen for a potentially serious injury, was afraid that he had forgotten Arabic. The next day Aladdin texted everyone saying he felt fine. In hindsight, this story is a comical illustration of every language learner's worst fear: losing the skills they worked so hard to acquire. As it turns out, Aladdin didn't forget Arabic and currently lives in Dubai.

A wise man once said, "Education is everything you remember from what you've been taught." I can't find the original author of the quote, but there's a lot of truth to it. It takes time to learn and even more time to completely forget. How much time? No one can know for certain. To my mind, staying current is the name of the game. However, it's reassuring to know that a few weeks or months of inactivity is unlikely to undo years of hard work.

Chapter 21

Having Clear Foreign Language Goals Maximizes Output

If you look around the room you are in right now, you will observe a great diversity of items, shapes, sizes, textures, colors, and functions, with all their associated nuances and subtleties. Every career, hobby, occupation, sport, industry, philosophy, plant, animal, object, event, and sensory experience–visual and otherwise–corresponds to a specific language. Language, in a word, is all-encompassing, and there are numerous registers, dialects, idioms, metaphors, and synonyms that express the same idea in multiple ways. "Mastering" one's native language is a lifelong pursuit. Mastering a foreign language is an even taller order.

The limits of my language mean the limits of my world. (Ludwig Wittgenstein)

As learners, we will never know everything in a foreign language (let perfectionism be gone), but the good news is that we won't ever have to.

A scholar of Classical Arabic doesn't need to know modern Arabic dialects. Someone who plans to live in Mexico likely won't get exposed to a lot of Caribbean Spanish. People learning French or German to read academic articles won't need to bother with the spoken language at all. During the first few years of language study, it makes sense to acquire as wide a language base as possible. For example, we may not need to know thousands of medical and legal terms, but it helps to know some of the more popular ones that are likely to surface. As I elaborated in chapter 3, most learners are advised to start with the standard variety of a language, since it will be relevant for school, print, media, the internet, and so forth. Once that foundation has been established, pivoting to dialects or subgenres of a language is a much more fluid process.

At first, I thought it would be enough just to master some survival phrases. But every time I met someone, they asked me questions I couldn't answer. So I learned more, until I could finally have a conversation. Then I wanted to have a longer, more interesting conversation, until eventually I realized what I really needed was to make

> *myself understood in both speech and writ-*
> *ing at roughly the same level I'm at in Eng-*
> *lish. In other words, even fluency wasn't*
> *enough. (See "Japan Today")*

Setting clear, achievable goals, on a short- and medium-term basis can keep the learner from feeling overwhelmed. For example, instead of trying to learn the classical, standard, and slang varieties of a language concurrently, it may make sense to focus on one or two of them at a time. Or, at the very least, to lengthen the time within which we expect to make significant progress. I have found that honing in on one dialect at a time, like Mexican or Puerto Rican Spanish; or one domain, like healthcare, law, or religion; or one focused book, like idioms and expressions, achieves this effect for me. This focus doesn't mean I'm not doing anything else in the language simultaneously; it just means I'm not biting off more than I can chew at any one time. The learner can devise processes that work for them based on what they are trying to get out of the language.

Language learning is often analogized to a journey. One of my earliest Spanish textbooks was entitled *¡Buen viaje!* (*Have a nice trip!*) I also like the analogy of an ocean. No one can plumb the depths of an ocean, certainly not within a few years. What language learners can do is become experts in the coves, creeks, and channels that make up their areas of interest or specialty.

Chapter 22

Context Is Key to Understanding Any Communication

"Context constitutes 90% of a message, words only 10%." (Abhijat Naskar)[19]

Context informs meaning and delimits the range of interpretive possibilities. It is the rope that keeps the reader or listener anchored to an accurate understanding of what is being communicated. We often don't think about context because it is second nature in most daily interactions. In an in-person gathering, for example, the shared environment is part and parcel of the context. Factors that influence the content of a dialogue include the weather, clothes, objects present in the room, the occasion for being together, and chronic markers like a shared cultural and educational background. Knowledge of context structures understanding; the more one knows about a context, the easier it is for them to interpret the intent and meaning of a speaker.

Imagine that you click on a Ted Talk entitled "Scientific Insights To Help You Get A Better

Night's Sleep." You can immediately infer from the formal event sponsor and title that the speaker is likely to employ standard conventions of the language. There's a clear thesis—getting a better night's sleep—which the speaker is likely to reference time and time again. The event is set in a particular city and is customarily marketed to a particular demographic. (*What is that demographic?*) The fact of a single speaker signifies that the listener needs to follow the logic, mood, and linguistic patterns of a sole individual. Or how about a sporting event? The audience knows that the lion's share of commentary is going to center on repetitive elements of the sport, like rules, gameflow, possession, and the same x number of players on either team. In the same way, the context for lectures, news programs, speeches, sermons, and advertisements tends to be relatively fixed and is knowable to those familiar with the genres. Once the context for a communication has been established, it is exponentially easier to arrive at understanding.

Now let's cite some examples where context is more elusive. Imagine watching a movie set in another country in another decade or century. A context this far-removed may pose some challenges to a modern viewer, depending on their historical and regional knowledge, even if the actors are communicating in a modern dialect. Now try treating that same movie as if it were an audiobook. In other words, listen, but don't watch. That task just became astronomically more difficult because you've been deprived of all visual context clues. The speakers are going to be addressing, alluding to, and cracking jokes about things they see, which don't need to be explicitly spelled out, that you will be hard-pressed to grasp without access to that information.

Now let's revisit the sports example from the previous paragraph. There's a reason why people who watch American football for the first time, native English speakers and foreigners alike, often have no idea what's going on, even if they can discern a lot of the individual words being spoken. Without context, sentences simply do not have a coherent meaning. It is common for people struggling to understand something at first to be able to do so rather effortlessly once the context has become clear.

Decoding Ancient Arabic Inscriptions

The Arab nomads of antiquity inscribed messages on rocks in an alphabet called Safaitic, the majority of which are found in modern-day Jordan, Syria, and Saudi Arabia. These messages consisted of genealogies, prayers, curses, eulogies, and simple narratives. I spent the summer of 2019 surveying these rocks in the Jordanian desert. As graduate students, our work basically entailed taking pictures of these messages to be deciphered by experts. I was not an expert, although I did take a course on The History of Arabic where we learned the alphabet and decoded several sample inscriptions. The hardest part about this process is the same challenge of understanding virtually every ancient text: a lack of context. This deficit relates to the general meaning of words (*what does this word denote?*), and to the meaning of words in full-form communications (*what does this word denote in this sentence?*).

Safaitic inscriptions happened to be formulaic, somewhat like the modern genres I referenced earlier in this chapter. This meant that there was a high degree of predictability, despite myriad linguistic and historical unknowns. On the flip side, many proposed translations turned out to be comical (and inaccurate) whenever they deviated too far from this context. This was especially true decades ago when not as much was known about this historical period or writing convention.

Knowledge of a history, culture, or domain illuminates context, as do environmental cues in more dynamic settings. It follows that by expanding our general knowledge base and heeding specific context clues, we can arrive at a more accurate understanding of speech or writing. In cases where we do not know the meaning of words, context can help us decipher them. In cases where we do know the meaning of words (or at least we *think* we do), it can insure against misunderstanding.

Chapter 23

Music, Comedy, and Dialogue Test
Advanced Listening Proficiency

"Listening is the skill that most of our students feel the least confident about and the least control over in terms of what they can do to improve. It is also the skill that is the most widely used, both in academic and non-academic contexts." (Christina Cole, University of Toronto)[20]

The term *mastery* is used to denote an advanced level of competency in a domain. However, mastery can be hard to define, let alone assess. While other trades and occupations–like chess, cosmetology, and carpentry–have standard criteria for becoming a *master* at the craft, no such benchmark exists in the world of language learning. I prefer the term *proficiency*, which seems a little less pretentious and lends itself better to nuance. Developing proficiency in each of the four basic language skills–reading, writing, speaking, and listening–presents unique challenges and opportunities. However, many learners struggle with listening, in particular. With listening, in contrast to reading, you aren't given access to the written form of the word and all that it entails. And, in contrast to speaking and writing, you do not have control over the content of communication. Among the ways to exercise listening proficiency, music, comedy, and dialogue stand out for their rigor. Music, comedy, and dialogue are characterized by nuance, fluidity, and abstraction that can give pause even to the most advanced speakers of a language. I proceed to address the challenges of these genres, in general terms, and conclude by sharing an excellent exercise that can be done at home to test—and improve—advanced listening proficiency.

A musical composition can center on any single theme or theme cluster. Given the short duration of most songs, the listener is in a time crunch to establish context and decipher meaning. Lyrics are often dictated by rhythm more so than clarity of communication. Rhyme, for example, is popular across multiple genres of music in numerous languages. The need to maintain a particular rhyme scheme can lead to non-standard word choices whose meaning is relatively difficult to make out. In addition, the value of lyrical music is not contained solely or primarily in the words. Many people, for example, enjoy listening to music for beats, rhythms, melodies, and harmonies, and the ability of music to induce an emotional change in state. It is also not uncommon for people to listen to music in a language they do not understand. Against this backdrop, singers do not have a duty to clearly articulate every syllable.

Music is also a highly artistic domain, where figures of speech, niche vocabulary, and creative, non-literal modes of expression abound (i.e. oral poetry). Most musicians create music with the understanding that fans will research the lyrics and repeat the same song multiple times. The need for the listener to "explore" to unpack layers of meaning may even be considered a virtue. Finally, the most obvious reason that lyrics can be hard to grasp is the music itself, which occupies the same space and competes for the listener's attention. On balance, music may require special cultural knowledge and an advanced language level to understand where one or a number of these complicating factors are at play.

Comedy, even more so than music, is pegged as one of the hardest genres of language to comprehend. Unlike music, comprehension, which is requisite for humor, *is* the goal; however, that comprehension can often be elusive. It's not just the fact that comedians use a lot of slang speech and vulgarity – both of which can be a challenge for people with a standard foreign language education. Moreso, the primary challenge of comedy lies in its characteristic subtlety of expression and cultural borrowing. Many jokes, for example, are based on puns or double entendres, where multiplex meanings of words enter into play. Classrooms are ill-suited for providing this depth of understanding

In addition, to be "in on the joke," the listener must possess insight into the culture in which it was birthed. Comedians are constantly telling stories that only people who have experienced similar things in life can relate to. Some themes are universal across time and place, whereas others involve local food, sports, traditions, celebrities, holidays, and shared cultural experiences from work, educational, and familial environments. Given that cultural products like these comprise the lion's share of speech, knowledge of them is as relevant to the language learner as grammar and vocabulary.

Finally, dialogue is the first and last frontier of language listening proficiency. While some dialogue is designed to be easy for beginners, many of the hardest speech productions assume this same form. First, a dialogue, by definition, consists of more than one speaker. In contrast to a lecture, sermon, news broadcast, or speech, dialogues feature a constant exchange of ideas between multiple parties. The listener must account for each of these parties and interpret their speech using things like past utterances, personality traits, linguistic habits, and emotional states as a guide. Second, dialogue that is heavily structured is the exception in life. There is a limited range of acceptable things for a lecturer, preacher, news broadcaster, and sports commentator to say. In these contexts, if the speaker deviates too far from the script, they can expect ridicule or be perceived as unprofessional. On the other hand, friends at a restaurant can literally talk about anything that fancies their interest.

In addition, dialogue between people, both in real life and media, features numerous references to "insider information" in the form of shared memories and past conversations. If the listener isn't privy to insider information, they can be at a loss to make sense of what the speakers are talking about. In sum, dialogue is dynamic, fast-paced, and open-ended. One might even argue that it is the most natural context for language. While dialogue performed by actors for an audience can be easier to understand, the fluidity of dialogue generally necessitates an advanced language level to make sense of in real time.

A Listening Proficiency Exercise Used by Professional Transcriptionists

If you want a practical activity to improve your listening, which can be used by beginners and advanced students alike, open a note on your phone or Word document. Load a short segment of speech in your target language (~1 minute or less starting out), taken from a song, comedy sketch, or live dialogue between characters. Your choice should be on your learning level, where you can make out at least some of its meaning, but not too easy where you aren't being challenged. You will also need access to the transcript so you can check your work. Transcripts are available for most songs as well as a lot of media on various streaming services. If there is a caption, heading, or description for the clip, resolve not to read it.

The next step is to play the audio and write down everything you hear. You can press pause or slow the audio down as needed to facilitate understanding and supply you with enough time to write. Professional transcriptionists are known for slowing down and speeding up audio to troubleshoot problem areas. For example, if you can't make out what is said at regular speed, you can slow the audio down to .5-.7, or speed it up to 1.1-1.3, in hopes that a change in perception might ring a bell. Sometimes it helps to play the full audio once, writing down what you can understand live. Then go back and adjust the speed as needed having made out more of the context.

Once the exercise is complete (don't take more than 10 minutes with this), compare your transcript to the official one. Make notes, mental or otherwise, of what you correctly transcribed, what you incorrectly transcribed, and what you couldn't make out at all. Then–and this step is important–go back and listen to the audio and compare it to the correct transcript. This exercise enables us to master the exact sounds that tripped us up. In many cases, you will be able to recognize the words in the official transcript, in which case the issue was purely auditory. As far as new words, it is harder to make out their sound than words we already know. While difficult, this a useful skill to develop. Auditorily making out new words enables us to look them up in a dictionary. The skill also sharpens our ear in the target language.

I used to listen to the same voices repeatedly from familiar arenas like academia, sports, and self-help. However, I realized I could hone my listening skills faster by pivoting to more difficult genres—like music, comedy, and dialogue—

and no longer treating speakers like a revolving door. Today, I occasionally like to play random clips on YouTube from unknown personalities, without reading the title or description, to see how much fine detail I can make out. The relative difficulty of this exercise demonstrates just how important context is for understanding, and how some genres can be especially difficult to master. In cases where a transcript is not available, we are limited in our ability to check our work, but we can often make out additional content with each subsequent listen. If I'm especially curious about a problematic segment, I will record it and send it to a native speaker to see what they are able to come up with.

In conclusion, active engagement with music, comedy, and dialogue can enhance critical listening skills and overall language proficiency. They are a resource that can be used to assess, and develop, the highest level of proficiency in the spoken variety of a language.

Chapter 24

Your Relationship to the Target Language Will Evolve

When I was in middle school, hearing Spanish spoken was like watching a magician perform a magic trick. Maybe it was the speakers' ability to seamlessly go back and forth between English and Spanish. Maybe it was the fact that meaningful communication was taking place and I hadn't a clue what was going on. *What were they saying?* The intellectual curiosity in me demanded to know. Most of my teachers and classmates did not speak Spanish, so the language had a confidential air to it. Or maybe it was the eloquent sound of the language itself. I imagined that if I could speak Spanish like my Latin American friends, life would be a lot more animated. At age 14, it was this seductive allure that motivated me to purchase a dry, tedious book on Spanish grammar from Barnes & Noble.

Fast-forward 14 more years, after countless hours of rigorous study and exposure, numerous language partners, professional training programs, a handful of dialects, and multiple bilingual jobs, my relationship to Spanish has evolved. It has gone from the glamorous honeymoon phase to a more mature dynamic grounded in reality. Indeed, the brain has a way of normalizing progress in an area. Capabilities formally idolized become the new baseline that the learner now takes for granted. We achieve one goal or scale one mountain, only to replace it with another. The goalposts, in other words, are constantly moving. To be sure, I am still fascinated by language, and knowing more than one enriches my life all the time. It has even become a part of my identity to the point that I cannot envision a version of myself that isn't bilingual or multilingual. I'm sure anyone who's ever invested a substantial amount of time in a hobby, skill, or pursuit can relate.

The more pride you have in a particular aspect of your identity, the more motivated you will be to maintain the habits associated with it. If you're proud of how your hair looks, you'll develop all sorts of habits to care for and maintain it. If you're proud of the size of your biceps, you'll make sure you never skip an upper-body workout. If you're proud of the scarves you knit, you'll be more likely to spend hours knitting each

> *week. Once your pride gets involved, you'll fight tooth and nail to maintain your habits. (James Clear in Atomic Habits)[21]*

Stories of experienced athletes and performers searching for an edge to stay on top of their game are a dime a dozen. The millionaire dollar question is *how does one avoid burnout and stay motivated with a single pursuit or occupation, day in and day out, for years on end?* As I discussed in chapter 5, passion is generally the most reliable source of motivation, while discipline is there to pick up the slack during times when it is lacking. Identification with the activity in question (*this is who I am*) and practical realities (*this is what I need to do* – e.g. target language jobs, relationships, or countries) work toward the same end of keeping the learner invested. Maybe the magic for you will never fade. Or maybe it will fade and you will need to rely on other creative sources of motivation–psychological, practical, or otherwise–to keep you on the path to achieving your goals.

Chapter 25

Foreign Language Study Is Not A Silver Bullet for the World's Problems

"Studying a foreign language expands one's worldview and limits the barriers between people: barriers cause distrust and fear. . . [It] teaches and encourages respect for other peoples: it fosters an understanding of the interrelation of language and human nature." (Auburn University's "Twenty-Five Reasons To Study A Foreign Language")[22]

"I find that people everywhere are similar as far as their experiences. They have the same aspirations in life. They face the same struggles. The only thing different is the language and culture." (Hala Batarseh)

"Not the ones speaking the same language, but the ones sharing the same feeling understand each other." (Rumi)

I firmly believe that if everyone took an interest in other cultures and languages, the world would be a more harmonious place. If people cannot have a conversation, how can they hope to understand one another? How can they hope to cooperate? In practice, I have also observed this to be the case. Many people who study foreign languages develop a love and affection for another culture or people group. They travel. They make friends. They come away with a better, more collaborative outlook than they had before. This has certainly been my experience. I agree with the sentiment quoted in the intro to this chapter. No matter where we go and what language we speak, the people we will encounter are a lot more alike than they are different. The implication is that the removal of language barriers can lead to mutual understanding and, simply put, make the world a better place.

I against my brother. I and my brother against my cousin. I, my brother, and my cousin against the world. (Arab Proverb)

However, all people who speak the same language do not get along. People have different worldviews, philosophies, and beliefs about the way things are and the way that things should be. And people have different interests due to political, economic, and environmental realities. I live in a country where everyone speaks English, and yet there is no shortage of conflict every single day. In addition, language study is not always undertaken by those with good intentions. Literature expanding on the imperative to "Know thy enemy," and "Know the language of thy enemy" illustrates this point. Many political leaders throughout history have used language and cultural knowledge to advance their private agendas rather than to build bridges and foster collaboration. In short, communication can't solve every problem, even under the best circumstances. While humanity's problems are deeper than language, foreign language knowledge can be a part of collective efforts to innovate, develop, and resolve conflict.

You Represent Your Country to the Target Language Population

Depending on where you're from, and what language you're studying, your target language population may not have much experience interacting with your nationality. Your target language population may look to you as an informal ambassador for insight, guidance, and representation on issues of country, culture, and language. On the other hand, there may be benefits or baggage associated with your country's political policies, both historical and present-day. While learners might prefer to treat language and culture in a vacuum, the political element is often inescapable.

CONCLUSION

My view is that we are living in the most exciting time in history to be studying a foreign language. The opportunity to travel and connect with people from all around the world is unprecedented. And the top-notch resources available to language learners, both online and in print, have accelerated the timeline of acquiring foreign language proficiency. Indeed, I have observed a marked improvement in the quality of these materials during the last decade, especially in the domain of colloquial speech. Long gone are the days of the old order when the learner had to look up words in paper dictionaries and consult in-person with a trusted source over every language-related difficulty. While it's possible today to work smarter than ever, language learning will always be a grind. As with any other skill, occupation, or hobby, we get out what we put in.

ABOUT THE AUTHOR

My journey with foreign languages began in high school when I was introduced to Latin culture through a friend and purchased a Spanish grammar book from Barnes & Noble. Fast-forward 15 years and I've spent a great deal of my life studying foreign languages (10+ years of Arabic and Spanish; 2+ years of Japanese and Latin; and < 1 year of French & German). I've lived in the Middle East, Tokyo, and DC, and worked multiple bilingual jobs, including my current one as a linguist in the American Midwest. Aside from being a language nerd, I enjoy blogging, web-making, hiking, and following professional sports.

REFERENCES

[1] Schwayder, Maya. "Change Languages, Shift Responses." Harvard Gazette, April 30, 2019. https://news.harvard.edu/gazette/story/2010/11/change-languages-shift-responses/.

[2] "How Many Languages Are There in the World?" Ethnologue, February 28, 2022. https://www.ethnologue.com/guides/how-many-languages.

[3] Schwartz, Barry. "The Paradox of Choice." TED, July, 2005. https://www.ted.com/talks/barry_schwartz_the_paradox_of_choice?language=en.

[4] Valuetainment. "Polyglot Who Speaks 20 Languages Reveals His Formula," YouTube Video, 26:46, February 5, 2021. https://www.youtube.com/watch?v=EVq6e5iaSQs

[5] "Foreign Language Training - United States Department of State." U.S. Department of State. Accessed June 11, 2022. https://www.state.gov/foreign-language-training/.

[6] "'Modern Family' Queer Eyes, Full Hearts." IMDb. Accessed June 11, 2022. https://www.imdb.com/title/tt4166966/characters/nm0005527.

[7] Peters, Ben. "Quote of the Day #230: Mastering a New Skill." Creator Villa, May 15, 2022. https://creatorvilla.com/quote-of-the-day-230-mastering-a-new-skill/.

[8] "FAQ: Language Acquisition." Linguistic Society of America. Accessed June 11, 2022. https://www.linguisticsociety.org/resource/faq-how-do-we-learn-language.

9 Carr, Brad. "Robert Greene on The Laws of Human Nature, Mastery, and Strategy," YouTube Video, 1:18:27, September 24, 2018. https://www.youtube.com/watch?v=64MsV-FECsY&t=0s.

10 Schawbel, Dan. "Robert Greene: How to Become the Master of Any Skill." Forbes, November 13, 2012. https://www.forbes.com/sites/danschaw-bel/2012/11/13/robert-greene-how-to-become-the-master-of-any-skill/?sh=355f8e121a23.

11 Talhouk, Suzanne. "Don't Kill Your Language." TED, December, 2012. https://www.ted.com/talks/su-zanne_talhouk_don_t_kill_your_language?language=en.

12 "2017 : What Scientific Term Or Concept Ought to Be More Widely Known?" Edge.org. Accessed June 11, 2022. https://www.edge.org/response-detail/27125.

13 "A Quote from Maxims and Reflections." Goodreads. Accessed June 11, 2022. https://www.goodreads.com/quotes/333723-those-who-know-nothing-of-foreign-languages-know-nothing-of.

14 "Screen Time Statistics: Average Screen Time in US vs. the Rest of the World." Comparitech, March 21, 2022. https://www.comparitech.com/tv-streaming/screen-time-statistics/.

15 "Language Proverbs And Sayings." Lewis University. Accessed June 11, 2022. https://www.lewisu.edu/academics/foreignlang/proverbs.htm.

16 Japan Today. "Why You Shouldn't Learn Japanese."

Japan Today, May 13, 2013. https://japan-today.com/category/features/opinions/why-you-shouldnt-learn-japanese.

[17] Raypole, Crystal. "How Many Thoughts Do You Have per Day?" Healthline, February 28, 2022. https://www.healthline.com/health/how-many-thoughts-per-day.

[18] "Negative Thinking: A Dangerous Addiction." Psychology Today, April 15, 2019. https://www.psychologytoday.com/us/blog/inviting-monkey-tea/201904/negative-thinking-dangerous-addiction.

[19] "Honor He Wrote Quotes by Abhijit Naskar." Goodreads. Accessed June 11, 2022. https://www.goodreads.com/work/quotes/94061687-honor-he-wrote-100-sonnets-for-humans-not-vegetables.

[20] Cole, Christina. "Why Teaching Second Language Listening Is Difficult and How to Use Bottom-up Listening Strategies to Teach Listening More Effectively." TESL Ontario, August 31, 2018. http://contact.teslontario.org/why-listening-is-hard/.

[21] "A Quote from Atomic Habits." Goodreads. Accessed June 11, 2022. https://www.goodreads.com/quotes/9536723-the-more-pride-you-have-in-a-particular-aspect-of.

[22] "25 Reasons to Study Foreign Languages." Auburn University College of Liberal Arts. Accessed June 11, 2022. https://cla.auburn.edu/world-languages/future-students/25-reasons-to-study-foreign-languages/.

Printed in Great Britain
by Amazon